JAGUAR MK 1 AND 2
with 240, 340 and Daimler derivatives

Other Titles in the Crowood AutoClassics Series

Jaguar Mk 1 and 2

with 240, 340 and Daimler derivatives

James Taylor

First published in 1995 by
The Crowood Press Ltd
Ramsbury, Marlborough
Wiltshire SN8 2HR

British Library Cataloguing-in-Publication Data
A catalogue record for this book is available from the British
Library

ISBN 1 85223 868 2

Picture Credits
All illustrations kindly supplied by the British Motor Industry Heritage Trust,
the Jaguar Daimler Heritage Trust, *Classic Cars* magazine, the National Motor
Museum at Beaulieu, Brooklands Books and Chris Horton.

Printed and bound by The Bath Press

Contents

Acknowledgements

A great deal has already been written about the Mk 1 and Mk 2 Jaguars, and that proved to be both a blessing and a problem when writing this book. It was a blessing, because I was able to cross-check material with that published by acknowledged Jaguar experts and to draw on their knowledge; and it was a problem, because the task of finding something new to say was correspondingly more difficult.

Thanks must go to a number of people in connection with this book. Help came in various forms from Anders Clausager at the British Motor Industry Heritage Trust, Simon Clay at the National Motor Museum at Beaulieu, Anne Harris at the Jaguar Daimler Heritage Trust, Paul Skilleter of *Jaguar World* magazine (which published some of the research incorporated in Chapter 3), Matt White at *Classic Cars* magazine and of course my friends at Brooklands Books. Last but certainly not least, thanks to the enthusiasts who made their cars available for inspection and photography: to Graham Bull (317CWP), Andrew Goddard (VPF806G), Vin Hammersley (Daimler under restoration), Carl James (MWK520G), Martin Payne (TLE793) and Benjamin Sill (BAR883F).

Jaguar Evolution

The Jaguar compacts and their times, 1955–1969

1955	Jaguar annouces the new 2.4-litre model
	Jaguar wins Le Mans with D-type sports racers
1956	William Lyons Knighted
	Jaguar D-type wins Le Mans for the second time
1957	Jaguar announces the 3.4-litre model
	2.4-litre Automatic becomes available
	Jaguar withdraws from works competition
1959	Jaguar announces the Mk 2 compacts
	Introducton of the Mini
1960	Demise of Armstrong-Siddeley after an unsuccessful attempt to complete with Jaguar's compacts
	Jaguar purchase of Daimler and associated companies
1961	Jaguar announces E-type and Mk 10 saloon
	Transport Minister Ernest Marples introduces the Ten-Year Test for all cars, forerunner of today's annual MOT test
1962	Jaguar announces Daimler 2.5-litre V8
	Ford announces Cortina (initially as Consul Cortina)
	BMC announces 1100
1963	Jaguar announces S-type
	Rover and Truimph announce new 2000 models
1965	Front seat saftey belts become compulsory on new cars in Britain
	Introduction of 'temporary' 70mph speed limit in Britain
	Rolls-Royce announces Silver Shadow, its first car with integral construction
1966	Jaguar announces 420 and Daimler Sovereign: Mk 10 renamed 420G
1967	Jaguar announces 240, 340 and Daimler V8-250 models
	MOT test became compulsory on three-year-old cars in Britain
1968	Last 340 Jaguars built
	Jaguar announces XJ6
1969	Last 240 Jaguars and Daimler V8-250s built

The Jaguar 2.4-litre Mk 1.

1 Jaguar Before the Compacts

When Jaguar introduced their compact saloons in 1955, the company was riding on the crest of a wave of success. Most important in that success had been the US market, where the company had been able to exploit the post-war fascination for European cars which would also make the fortunes of MG, Triumph and others.

To a considerable extent, that success helped to shape the basic parameters of the new compact saloons. Despite the radically new (for Jaguar) engineering which went into them, they had to conform to public expectations of the Jaguar marque. It is therefore impossible to understand the factors which conditioned them without first being aware of what the buying public expected of Jaguar back in 1955.

Jaguar's range for the year which preceded the compacts' introduction consisted of two basic models. On the one hand was the large Mk VII saloon, and on the other was the XK120 sports car, available in either open or closed forms. The Mk VII was a large luxury saloon, offering spacious accommodation with a traditionally British wood and leather interior, while the XK120 was a stylish and charismatic two-seater. In many respects, they were as different as chalk and cheese and yet they had three very important factors in common: pricing, performance and good looks. It was these three characteristics which defined the Jaguar marque for the motoring public of 1955.

It had always been Jaguar's policy to keep prices as low as possible, both in order to undercut competitors and to promote an image of value for money. In this, the Mk VII and XK120 were fully representative of the Jaguar tradition. The Mk VII was essentially a 'poor man's Bentley', and in 1954 its basic retail price, inclusive of taxes, was £1,616. The cheapest Bentley then available cost around three times as much. As for the XK120, which was similarly priced, its most obvious rivals came from the likes of Ferrari and Aston Martin, and all of them were vastly more expensive than the Jaguar.

High performance was also a Jaguar trademark, and the company had furthered its image in that field with a spectacular series of successes in international motorsport during the 1950s. First had come the C-type sports racers (strictly known as XK120C models), which had won the Le Mans 24-hour road race in 1951 and again in 1953. Then in 1954 had come the D-type, which won at Le Mans in the early summer of 1955. But perhaps the most important aspect of these and other sporting victories, as far as Jaguar customers were concerned, was that the sports racers depended on race-tuned derivatives of the same engine which powered both the Mk VII saloons and the XK120 sports cars.

That engine – the XK twin overhead camshaft six-cylinder – had first appeared in 1948 and would not finally go out of production until more than forty years later. In road-going 3.4-litre form, it endowed the beefy Mk VII saloon with a top speed of 103mph (165km/h), while the XK120 laid claim to 120mph (193km/h) or more. For the early 1950s, this kind of performance was the stuff of which dreams were made: the average family saloon of the time struggled to reach 70mph (112km/h).

Both the big Mk VII and the XK120 were strikingly styled cars. Bulky though it undoubtedly was, the saloon looked elegant thanks to its graceful curves and sweeping wing-lines. It had a special sort of presence which was lacking in other saloons of its day, and when parked alongside the rather upright Bentleys and Armstrong-Siddeleys of the early 1950s, it appeared low and streamlined. By contrast, it looked upright and traditional alongside contemporary American machinery, but that very conservatism distinguished it from the crowd and endeared it to wealthy Americans.

As for the XK120, its long and low lines – reminiscent of the sleek pre-war BMW sports cars – stood out in any company. Once again, graceful curves and sweeping wing-lines were the distinguishing features, and the Jaguar could hold its head up in the company of any Italian exotics from the styling houses of Pininfarina, Vignale, Touring or Zagato. Across the Atlantic, the only additional competition for the XK120 came from the Chevrolet Corvette, which at this stage did not yet have the attractive lines for which the marque would later become known.

THE ORIGINS

In fact, it had been styling more than any other factor which had been Jaguar's roots. Back in the early 1920s, William Walmsley had moved his small motorcycle sidecar business from Stockport to Blackpool and

there he had met and entered into partnership with the younger William Lyons. Walmsley's sidecars were notable for their elegant design, and the enthusiastic Lyons developed his eye for a good line from Walmsley's example. In 1922 they jointly formed the Swallow Sidecar Company, and their business was so successful that they were able as early as 1926 to branch out into making car bodies.

These car bodies had styling which was as distinctive and elegant as the styling of the sidecars, but Swallow stuck to a policy of offering bodies for relatively cheap cars. Thus, where many coachbuilders preferred to work with luxury models, Swallow instead provided special coachwork for

Jaguar's origins were in the Swallow sidecar business, which offered stylish products such as this 1922 model, seen fitted to a contemporary Douglas motorcycle.

more mundane cars, primarily the Austin Seven. This made their cars attractive to the customer who could not afford an expensive luxury car but who nevertheless wanted something which stood out from the crowd of lesser models. In this early experience lay the origins of the market positioning which Jaguar cars would later adopt.

One important factor in Swallow's success was of course pricing, and by adopting quite sophisticated production processes they were able to minimize the cost of making their bodies. So it was that, when the growth of their business forced them to seek larger premises, they looked carefully at how best to use this opportunity to minimize costs further. One overhead which they had been unable to control was the cost of transporting chassis to Blackpool from the Midlands heart of the motor industry; and they had already recognized that it was easier to recruit skilled staff in the Midlands than in Blackpool. The solution was therefore obvious: Swallow would move to the Midlands. And so the company moved to premises at Foleshill, in Coventry, in the autumn of 1928.

Expansion continued. Lyons introduced further new production methods and before Christmas 1928 had pushed the rate of

Typical of the special coachwork turned out by Swallow was this stylish saloon body on a 1931 Austin 7. The grille bears the legend, 'Austin Swallow'.

production up from twelve car bodies a week to fifty. The sidecar activities meanwhile continued. Over the next three years, Swallow also tackled further types of chassis, including Fiat, Swift and – most notably – Standard. In all cases, their combination of attractive lines and striking paintwork completely transformed the perpendicular look of the originals, and created cars which were genuinely different from others available on the market in Britain. Mechanically, however, they were unmodified. The next logical step for Swallow was to start building cars which were mechanically as well as bodily different from anything which could be bought elsewhere, and in 1931 they took that step.

THE FIRST SS MODELS

The new models which Swallow announced in October 1931 are often described as the company's first complete cars, although to call them that is really overstating the case. Standard, content with the special bodies Swallow had been offering on their chassis since 1928, had agreed to supply Swallow with their 16hp and 20hp engines, fitted at the Standard works into a special chassis designed to meet Swallow's requirements. The key to this chassis was that it was much lower than those normally fitted to saloons of the period, which enabled Swallow to clothe it with rakish new sporting bodywork.

It was William Lyons, always the front man at Swallow, who had secured Standard's agreement, and it was he who had persuaded them to allow the new car to be badged as an SS. The exact significance of the letters never was resolved, but the significance of the new name was that Swallow now had a marque of their own. The SSI, as the 16hp car was called, was accompanied by an altogether smaller new

model based on the Standard Little Nine. Even though this was more in the vein of Swallow's earlier rebodying efforts, it was also badged as an SS – in fact, an SSII – and this development made fairly clear what Swallow's next move was likely to be.

Sure enough, in 1933 Lyons and Walmsley set up a new company which they called SS Cars Ltd. From then on, Lyons' primary objective was to establish the company as a credible builder of complete cars. Styling remained important, and the later SS models were offered with a variety of attractive bodies. Road performance to match that styling was also important, and SS took full advantage of Standard's engine developments in the first half of the 1930s. Re-designs made the SSI and SSII much better cars, and by 1935 SS had become established as a small-volume maker of stylish sporting cars costing rather less than their exotic looks suggested.

WATERSHED – THE SS JAGUARS

By this stage, high performance had become a very important ingredient in Lyons' vision of SS Cars. As Standard had nothing in the offing which was likely to fit his future requirements, he turned to tuning expert Harry Weslake and asked him to develop the big Standard engine for more power. Weslake's solution was to re-design the top end of the engine with a new cylinder head and overhead valves instead of side valves, and Lyons somehow managed to persuade Standard to manufacture this revised engine exclusively for SS Cars.

However, Lyons wanted more. The new engine needed to go with a new body, and for the new body it would be necessary to design a new chassis. The bodywork was something he was more than capable of tackling himself, but there was no one at the

The rakish lines of this travel-stained SSI hinted at much more expensive machinery in the early 1930s.

Foleshill works who had any experience of designing chassis. So it was that SS Cars took their first proper engineer on to the staff in April 1935. William Heynes, who joined the company from Humber, was later to become a central figure in the Jaguar story.

It was October 1935 when the new car was ready. Seeking to give it a new name, Lyons had settled for Jaguar, after the First World War Armstrong-Siddeley aero engine which had interested him many years earlier. And so the new SS Jaguars went on sale for 1936, a range of sleek sports saloons and open four-seater tourers. In addition, there was a new short-wheelbase two-seater

sports model called the SS90 – an important model in its own right because it was the first proper sports car from the company. The saloons could be obtained with either the 1,608cc four-cylinder side-valve Standard engine as 1.5-litre models or with the Weslake-developed 2,664cc six-cylinder engine as 2.5-litre models, while the open cars came only with the larger engine. For the moment, SSI and SSII models remained available alongside the newcomers, but they were soon dropped.

Towards the end of 1935, William Walmsley left SS Cars and joined a caravan manufacturer in Coventry. The split appears to have been amicable, and

The first cars to bear the Jaguar name were introduced in 1935. This sleek and stylish saloon is a 1936 SS Jaguar 2.5-litre, pictured during preparations for that year's Paris Motor Show.

probably resulted from Walmsley's desire to avoid the complications and stresses of running a large company such as SS Cars seemed set to become. With his departure, SS Cars was floated as a public company, and thereafter was obliged to have its own board of directors who met at regular intervals. Although SS Cars Ltd did have a board of directors, its meetings were more of a legal formality than anything else: in reality, Lyons now took over the running of the company.

For 1937 the SS Jaguars were further improved, but the major changes came in the autumn of that year when the 1938 models were announced. For a start, the traditional coachbuilt saloon bodies with their wooden frames had been replaced by all-steel bodyshells of similar appearance

which were both lighter and cheaper to produce; and these had been joined by a new wooden-framed drophead coupé body which added to the SS marque's upper-crust pretensions. The 1.5-litre engine, too, had been reworked and now sported overhead valves which gave it much more performance than the old side-valve engine.

In addition, there was a sleek new sports tourer called the SS100, available with either the 2.5-litre engine or a new 3.5-litre type which was also available in the saloons and drophead coupés. Although this was in fact yet another development of the Standard six-cylinder, and was once again made exclusively for SS Cars by Standard, it was still the closest the Foleshill company had yet come to an engine they might call their own.

Little had changed eleven years later! This is a 1947 2.5-litre saloon. It belonged to Colonel Rixon Bucknall, and had covered 150,000 miles by the time it was pictured in 1961 at Beaulieu, now the home of the National Motor Museum.

WARTIME

By the time war broke out in 1939, the SS Jaguars had already established a formidable reputation. At home, they had been eagerly adopted by the sporting fraternity and there was even an SS Car Club for enthusiastic owners. Looking back rather wistfully in 1944, Montagu Tombs of *The Autocar* magazine described the cars of the late 1930s as 'capable of providing an outstanding performance on the road, and offering exceptional value'. Yet the SS Jaguars were by no means common: by the time the Foleshill factory ceased car manufacture and turned over to the production of war matériel in 1940, just 14,383 had been built in five seasons. And of the earlier SSI

and SSII models, there had been no more than 6,029 examples.

When the war came, SS Cars were poised on the brink of further expansion. Production had increased enormously to meet the rising demand during 1938–9, and 1939 had seen a record output of 5,320 cars. Most popular of all was the steel-bodied 1.5-litre saloon, which accounted for over 60 per cent of the total. During 1939 William Lyons had bought Motor Panels, one of SS Cars' suppliers of body parts. His intention had been that SS Cars should be able to manufacture their own bodies entirely in-house, which would of course have minimized costs and would also have afforded the company greater flexibility in the manufacture of their bodies.

However, the expansion never took place. Like every other motor manufacturer, SS Cars were obliged to respond to the needs of the armed services. The Foleshill plant started to turn out aircraft parts, took on aircraft repair work, and in 1944 designed and built some experimental lightweight miniature jeeps intended to be carried in transport aircraft and parachuted into action. The Swallow Sidecar Company, meanwhile – which still existed as an SS subsidiary – took care of the entire requirements of the Army, Royal Navy and Royal Air Force for motorcycle sidecars.

There was, therefore, little time to spare for thinking about new car designs or improving the standing of the company. In fact, the war proved a major setback for SS Cars, and Lyons was obliged to sell Motor Panels shortly after hostilities ended for the simple reason that SS Cars could not afford to keep it on and expand as they had planned six years earlier. The Swallow Sidecars subsidiary was also sold off during 1945 in order to raise capital.

In the meantime, Standard had dropped a bombshell with the announcement that they did not wish to resume production of special engines on behalf of SS Cars when the war was over. Fortunately for the smaller company, they were quite prepared to sell the tooling for the 2.5-litre and 3.5-litre six-cylinder engines, and at an advantageous price. Lyons seized this opportunity with both hands and by the middle of 1945 the redundant Standard tooling had been installed at SS Cars' Foleshill plant to give the company its very own engine at last. Tooling for the 1.5-litre engines meanwhile remained in Standard's possession, and in fact the engine soon reappeared in cars from Triumph, which had been bought out by Standard as the war drew to a close.

There was one final change at Foleshill before car production resumed over the summer of 1945. The initials 'SS' had taken on unfortunate associations during the war years, as they were used by Nazi Germany's crack troops. Clearly, with sour memories of SS brutality lingering in the minds of British citizens, any company bearing those initials was likely to be shunned. So at an Extraordinary General Meeting in March 1945, William Lyons had his company's name changed to Jaguar Cars. It was the logical choice and a happy one.

THE LATE 1940s

The British economy had been shattered by the immense cost of the war and the Government of the day saw as its clear priority putting that economy back on a sound footing. This could only be achieved by a combination of austerity measures to limit consumption at home with an emphasis on foreign trade to earn revenue abroad.

The car makers, in consequence, were encouraged to build cars primarily for export, and the Government ensured that they would comply by rationing sheet steel and allocating it in quantity only to those companies which could show a good export performance. For Jaguar, the need to export was an entirely new concept; although a few cars had been exported in the late 1930s, the company had been able to sell all it produced on the home market and had therefore never gone to the trouble and expense of setting up overseas distribution networks. But now, it had to.

Like the majority of other British car makers, Jaguar started production after the war with cars which were essentially little changed from those they had been making when production had been halted in 1940. Standard had agreed to resume supplies of the 1.5-litre engine for the time being (although post-war versions differed from the pre-war types), and so a full range of three engines was available. The first bodies were all saloons, however; drophead coupé bodies did not become available again until December 1947 and then only with the six-cylinder engines; and the SS100 open tourer was never revived.

It was typical of Britain's insularity, even in the second half of the 1940s, that Jaguar should have thought only in terms of right-hand-drive cars for export. The company had never built left-hand-drive cars before the war, and seems to have resisted the idea as long as possible. However, new and promising markets like the USA were only prepared to put up with right-hand-drive cars as a novelty for a limited period. Exports to the USA started in January 1947 and by August that year Jaguar had been forced to capitulate and start making left-hand-drive models.

However, Jaguar had no intention of continuing to develop the pre-war 1.5-litre, 2.5-litre and 3.5-litre models for much longer. With his original plans for Jaguar's expansion in the early 1940s in ruins, Lyons had begun during the war years to think of the new car which would eventually take over from the SS Jaguar range. Most importantly, he wanted his new saloon to be a genuine 100mph (160km/h) car (a 1939 3.5-litre saloon was capable of about 92mph/148km/h), and that meant he would need a new engine. For maximum power, he thought it should have the twin-ohc configuration which had at that time only been seen in racing engines and in exotic machinery, and which was widely believed to be too complicated to produce economically and too difficult for the average garage mechanic to service and maintain.

So it was that Lyons began to discuss with his engineers ways of achieving what he wanted. The design target was 160bhp, which had been achieved for brief periods with a highly-tuned 3.5-litre engine in an SS100 in 1939, and the discussions mostly took place while Lyons and others were on fire-watching duties at night in the Foleshill factory. Chief among those involved were William Heynes, Walter Hassan, and newcomer Claude Baily, who had joined SS Cars from Morris on the outbreak of war; but Harry Weslake was also consulted about the design of the cylinder head and combustion chambers. The work started in earnest during 1943 and the first experimental engines were four-cylinder types. In due course, however, a satisfactory design was developed and Jaguar built a six-cylinder prototype. In the form eventually adopted for production, this displaced 3,442cc and put out exactly 160bhp – which had been its design target.

However, Lyons decided against putting the new XK engine into his existing models. Such an exciting new engine, he believed, needed to be shown off in something more interesting than a warmed-over pre-war saloon. So he decided that the new 100mph (160km/h) saloon should be a completely new car, with new chassis, suspension and body as well as the new engine. Work on the new body design quickly demonstrated that it would need large pressings which were beyond Jaguar's own panel-making capabilities at that stage. So Lyons turned to Pressed Steel, who were happy to accept the contract but needed a year to tool-up for the new saloon body.

Meanwhile, Jaguar needed to do something about their current range of cars, because even the seller's market of the late 1940s could not be expected to tolerate pre-war designs indefinitely. By 1947 many other manufacturers had come up with new designs, and these were making the Jaguars look increasingly old-fashioned. To bridge the gap and keep interest in the marque alive until the new saloon was ready for production, Lyons therefore decided to develop the existing saloons further – and to show off his new XK engine in a striking-looking sports car.

17

For the new saloon, Lyons had the chassis stiffened and equipped with a torsion-bar independent front suspension in place of the old leaf-spring type. He drew up a new body, broadly similar to that on the existing cars but markedly more modern in appearance, and he made sure that this body could be built in the traditional way at Foleshill. The result was a much heavier car than those it was to replace and that was one reason why the new Mk V Jaguar (as it was called) came only with the six-cylinder 2.5-litre and 3.5-litre engines. One other reason for the absence of a 1.5-litre version was no doubt that Lyons no longer wished to depend on Standard for one of his power plants.

The Mk V Jaguar was announced in October 1948, at Britain's first post-war Motor Show. Available in both saloon and drophead coupé forms, it was an elegant if unspectacular car, of which most examples went abroad to help Britain's export drive. Lyons knew he had bought time in order that his new 100mph (160km/h) saloon could be honed to perfection, but he probably had little idea just how important Jaguar's second new model at the 1948 Motor Show was going to be. That car was called the XK120.

In the Jaguar scheme of things, the XK120 sports car was a belated replacement for the pre-war SS100. It was not really intended for long-term production, more as an image-builder; but like the Land Rover which had reached the market earlier that year and had been intended as a stop-gap, it

Although a wider radiator grille and other touches updated the appearance of the 1948 Mk V Jaguar, the car was unmistakably a warmed-over pre-war design. This car had the new torsion-bar independent front suspension but the old pushrod engine. That curved trailing edge to the rear window would be a Jaguar saloon trademark for more than twenty years.

The sleek lines of the XK120 made it a winner from the start, although it must be said that the roadster top was rather crude.

was destined to have a much longer production life.

The XK120 had a shortened version of the new Mk V saloon chassis, clothed with sleek and streamlined two-seater bodywork styled as usual by Lyons and clearly inspired by the 1940 BMW 328 Mille Miglia cars. That alone was attractive enough to have guaranteed its sales success, but in addition the car became the showcase for the new 3.4-litre six-cylinder XK engine. In the light sports car body, this gave extraordinary performance for the time, and the XK120 went on to become a major export success. By the time it was superseded by the rather better developed but generally similar XK140 in 1954, more than 12,000 examples had been built.

THE 100MPH SALOON

The Mk V soldiered on for two years before Jaguar's new saloon was ready to be launched, but all those who saw the new car at the 1950 London Motor Show would surely have agreed that it was worth the wait. The car's flowing lines echoed those of the XK120; the 3.4-litre XK engine offered a top speed of more than 100mph (160km/h); and somehow, Jaguar had managed to keep the basic price below £1,000 – the figure above which cars attracted a higher rate of Purchase Tax. Jaguar had called it the Mk VII, deliberately skipping a number after the Mk V because the contemporary Bentley was known as the Mk VI.

The car's pricing was hugely attractive, but it was of largely academic interest to British car buyers because the Mk VII was intended initially for export only. In pursuit of that aim, Jaguar whisked the London Motor Show car across to New York as soon as the show ended and there the car was accorded a reception perhaps even more rapturous than the one it had received in

The first proper post-war Jaguar saloon was the Mk VII of 1950. It was also the first Jaguar saloon to feature the XK engine.

Exports became increasingly important to Jaguar as the 1940s came to an end. This picture shows Mk V saloons on the quayside at Southampton, waiting to be loaded on board the transatlantic liner Mauretania.

The XK120C, or C-type, was the first of Jaguar's great sports-racers of the 1950s. This is the car, driven by Tony Rolt and Duncan Hamilton, which won at Le Mans in 1953. Disc brakes gave it a decisive advantage over the opposition.

London. Within three days, Jaguar took orders for no fewer than 500 cars in the USA. Following the success of the XK120 sports car, Jaguar had now definitively broken into the market which would soon become their largest single source of income.

Demand for the Mk VII and the XK120 built up so quickly that Jaguar's Foleshill premises were bursting at the seams by 1951. They were very fortunate that year to be able to purchase a redundant Daimler plant at Browns Lane, near Coventry, and to move their entire manufacturing operation there. It was a good thing they did, for demand would continue to expand, led by the US market.

It was US demand which led to the introduction in 1953 of an optional automatic transmission for the Mk VII Jaguar. Next came an overdrive, more popular in Europe.

Then in the autumn of 1954, at the same time as the XK120 became an XK140, came the substantially revised Mk VIIM with more powerful engine, new bumpers and a host of minor but significant improvements. And all the time Jaguar's reputation was growing along with production volumes. Before the introduction of the XK120 and Mk VII, Jaguar's annual production figures had hovered at a little over 4,000; by 1954, with both models selling strongly in the USA and home-market sales on the increase now that restrictions had eased, the annual totals were regularly hovering around the 10,000 mark.

This improvement in Jaguar's fortunes had far-reaching effects, for without it there is little doubt that the company would not have been able to finance the design, development and introduction of the new compact models which appeared in 1955.

2 Life and Times of the Compact Jaguars

The fourteen-year production life of the compact Jaguars spanned one of the most interesting and exciting periods in the evolution of the British motor industry. In many ways, the second half of the 1950s and the decade which followed represented a golden age for that industry, when cars were affordable and in plentiful supply, when British cars were still respected all over the world, and when imported machinery still accounted for only a tiny proportion of all new cars sold in Britain. And in many ways, the compact Jaguar saloons came to symbolize that golden age better than any other cars of their time.

Yet the Jaguar company underwent enormous changes in those fourteen years. When the new 2.4-litre Jaguar was announced in 1955, the company which built it was enjoying unprecedented success; success in the USA, where booming export sales were helping to fill the company coffers, and success in the popular imagination, as Jaguar's international racing victories helped to bolster the image of Britain as invincible. By 1969 Jaguars were still one of Britain's proudest exports and the company still built cars which were the envy of other manufacturers worldwide. But the racing victories were now many years in the past, for Jaguar had not fielded a works team for twelve years.

What was more, Jaguar was no longer the proudly independent company it had been in 1955, for in 1966 it had joined forces with the British Motor Corporation, and then two years later had become part of the amorphous conglomerate known as British Leyland. As yet, British Leyland had not sunk to the depths it would reach in the middle 1970s, but there were already signs that all was not running as smoothly as the political architects of the merger might have hoped.

THE MOTORING WORLD IN THE LATER 1950s

As peace returned to Britain after the Second World War, the Government introduced a number of measures to help rebuild the country's economy. Among these were several which affected the motor industry: it was obliged to build primarily for export and thus to bring revenue into the country, while import taxes and other restrictions would ensure that foreign manufacturers would be unable to compete seriously with it on the home market. These measures promoted a kind of insularity within the industry which gave it a character all of its own, and even by the end of the 1950s the British motoring scene was infused with a kind of blinkered patriotism which was perhaps more appropriate to the 1930s.

One result of the situation was that British manufacturers were not obliged to compete with foreign products at home. As they rarely encountered foreign cars abroad because their exports were largely into closed markets in the Commonwealth, they tended to build cars which were ideally suited to British towns and A-roads but which were not up to the rigours of high-speed use on German Autobahns or to prolonged exposure to the unmade roads of Africa. In due course, this would lead to problems as the Commonwealth shrank, as British car makers tried to find new export markets to compensate, and as restrictions on foreign imports were eased at the end of the decade.

Where most British manufacturers lagged behind was in engine design. Side-valve engines were still common in the 1950s, and only a few makers took the risk of introducing the high-revving overhead-valve designs which were gradually becoming the norm elsewhere. Low gearing coupled with low-revving engines meant that many British cars lacked the high-speed cruising ability of some of their Italian or German counterparts, and to meet the demand for higher cruising speeds, several manufacturers now offered overdrive transmissions. Even Jaguar, whose twin-ohc engines were among the most advanced in the industry, chose to provide overdrive as an optional extra. No doubt this was as much because the customers expected it as because it was really necessary.

By the middle 1950s, car buyers were also increasingly demanding automatic transmissions. These had been popular in the USA for many years, but most types available had been unsuitable for use with the smaller and less torquey engines which were the norm in Europe. In Britain, however, Jaguar were among the leaders in this field, both because their engines were larger than the norm and because their strong export sales in the USA had made it imperative to offer an automatic option.

Unitary construction was gradually taking over in the British motor industry, although there were still many cars built with separate chassis and body structures during the 1950s. Most large cars – Rovers, Rolls-Royces and Jaguars among them – still depended on a separate chassis; and the traditional British sports car also had a separate chassis until the very end of the decade. Unitary construction was still generally reserved for smaller cars, makers being unwilling to risk it on larger vehicles until stress engineering was better understood.

Even so, the future was looking rosy for Britain's motor industry in 1955, when Jaguar introduced their new compact saloon. British manufacturers had established strong export markets for their products, and there was no reason to think that demand should fall off in the foreseeable future. The shortages of cars on the home market, caused by Government insistence on priority for exports, were now easing as production increased and the general economic situation improved. In short, Britain's motor industry was booming, and in 1955 Britain could boast that it was second only to the USA in the numbers of cars it built annually. These were good times for Jaguar, too, and shortly after the introduction of the 2.4-litre models, its Chairman William Lyons became Sir William Lyons, his knighthood being bestowed for Jaguar's success in export markets.

Production continued to rise for the next few years, and so did demand on the home market. In 1956 the British motor industry built 707,000 cars, in 1958 it passed the one million mark for the first time ever, and production would keep on rising until it peaked in 1964. Some half a million new cars were being registered in Britain every year in the middle 1950s, and this figure rose steadily to reach 820,000 in 1960. Thereafter, it continued to rise.

Things were already beginning to change,

though: in 1956 Britain slid suddenly from second to fourth in the league table of world motor manufacturing nations. The USA remained in first place, but West Germany had taken the number two position and France had slipped in at number three. Britain would never again be among the top three. British complacency was also shaken by the Suez crisis of 1956, which was followed by six months of petrol rationing and a consequent slump in new-car sales. Worse, foreign manufacturers began to look with greater interest at the British market towards the end of the decade, anticipating the relaxation from 1959 of the Government's import restrictions. Things could never be quite the same again.

ENTER THE NEW JAGUAR

Into all this, the 2.4-litre Jaguar was born in 1955, and it is not hard to understand why it made such an impact. For a start, it was a relatively large car to have unitary construction at that stage. Secondly, it brought a high-revving, high-performance engine into a new and lower price bracket. Thirdly, it offered the expected option of an overdrive to suit both export markets and the increasing numbers of Britons who took their cars to the European continent on holiday. Lastly, it was still very much a British car, with traditional leather upholstery and a wooden facia which might have been taken from any one of a dozen 1930s designs.

Two examples of the new 2.4-litre saloon were displayed at the 1955 London Motor Show, alongside the company's Mk VII saloons and XK140 sports models.

For Britain, it was an ideal car – fast, relatively agile and handily sized. For Jaguar's export markets, however, it had some drawbacks, most notably in the USA, where it was seen as simply not fast enough. Nor did it show up well in Germany against similar-sized Mercedes-Benz models. So the introduction of a much more powerful model with Jaguar's well respected 3.4-litre engine in 1957 came not a moment too soon.

In truth, however, the 3.4 was not ready for production when it was announced early in 1957, initially for export only. While its acceleration and top speed were beyond reproach, and its handling and roadholding at least as good as could be expected at the time, its brakes were distinctly marginal for such a powerful car. Jaguar would probably have liked to fit it with disc brakes from the beginning, but the new brakes were not ready in time and so the first cars retained an all-drum braking system. Nevertheless, Jaguar could still claim to be among the leaders in automotive engineering when they finally did introduce disc brakes on the production cars later in 1957. They had, after all, been using disc brakes on their sports-racers for several years, and they could effectively discount the only two other production cars then using disc brakes. The pioneer – Citroën's 1955 DS19 – hardly counted in Britain because it was a strange foreign concoction, while the Triumph TR3 which had been disc-braked since 1956 was a sports car rather than a saloon!

JAGUAR IN THE LATE 1950s

While the 2.4-litre and 3.4-litre Jaguars were selling in increasing numbers to enthusiastically appreciative buyers in the second half of the 1950s, many important changes were taking place at Jaguar. Among them were the cessation of direct factory participation in competition and an increase in demand which caused Jaguar to require additional production space for the second time in ten years.

It was in October 1956 that Jaguar announced the closure of its competitions department. The reason given in the official statement was simple: the company's engineering staff was heavily committed to work on forthcoming new models and running a competitions department was simply too demanding of their time. Whether or not that was the whole truth has never been clear, but Jaguar certainly were busy by the end of 1956.

By then they would have been working not only on the 3.4-litre compact saloon and its disc brakes (both for 1957 introduction) but also on automatic transmissions for both 2.4 and 3.4 compacts, and on the improvements which would turn the big Mk VIIM saloon into a Mk VIII and the XK140 sports model into an XK150 during the same year. Then there was the road-going XK-SS version of the D-type sports-racer, and work must also have been under way on the forthcoming 3.8-litre version of the XK engine, which would appear in 1959 in the XK150, the Mk 2 versions of the compact saloons, and the Mk IX successor to the Mk VIII. In the planning stages there were probably also the modifications which would turn the original compact Jaguars into Mk 2 versions in 1959. After that there would be the all-new Mk X saloon and the E-type …

Speculation that Jaguar might have resumed competition activity in 1958 therefore seems rather like wishful thinking, but in any case whatever hopes there may have been were to be dashed early in 1957. On the evening of 12th February – just two weeks before the new 3.4-litre compacts were due to be released – a major fire broke out at the factory. The damage caused was estimated at £3.5 million; nearly half of the main

More power, especially for the US market, came in 1957 when the 3.4-litre engine was put into the compact bodyshell. This is the car on the Jaguar stand at the London Motor Show that year.

factory was destroyed and with it went several hundred cars. Most severely affected were the service, trim and final test areas, but fortunately none of the production tooling was damaged. As a result, the disruption to car production was minimal; the lines were running again within nine days and were back to normal within six weeks.

This was undoubtedly a serious setback for Jaguar, but in some ways the fire could not have occurred at a better time. The last months of 1956 and the early months of 1957 were plagued by petrol shortages in the wake of the Suez crisis which had erupt-

ed the previous autumn, and the sales of big and thirsty cars were in the doldrums. Browns Lane had in fact been working only a four-day week between November and January to avoid building more cars than it could sell. Sales did eventually recover during the summer of 1957, by which time Jaguar too were back in business. And that business continued to expand – so much so that by the end of the decade, Jaguar had run out of space at Browns Lane, the factory which on its acquisition in 1951 had seemed to answer all their prayers for more space at their old Foleshill premises.

Mk VIIs and compact saloons wait for the insurance assessor and then the scrap man at Browns Lane after the fire which burned out the northern third of the works in February 1957.

Jaguar re-established production very quickly after the fire. The damage it caused is still in evidence in this picture, but 2.4-litre and 3.4-litre models are once again passing down the assembly lines.

The 3.4-litre model was the cause of considerable excitement in the motoring world. Few cars could reach such high speeds, and very few of those could seat five passengers in comfort. This is an early left-hand-drive automatic model which was road-tested by The Motor *in 1957.*

The 3.4-litre engine made the compact saloon into a real road-burner, although the car cried out for the disc brakes which lagged a little behind its introduction. This is a very early example, with straps over the air cleaner – these were later deleted to give the neat underbonnet so typical of all Jaguars in this period.

THE MK 2 MODELS

Jaguar took seriously the criticisms which had been made of their original compact Jaguars, and the number of minor improvements made during their production lifetime made the final cars into rather better machines than the original ones had been. However, some of the criticisms demanded more fundamental revisions of the basic design and these revisions were all revealed together during 1959 in the new cars which Jaguar called the Mk 2 models. The earlier cars, with Jaguar's blessing, then took on the retrospective 'Mk 1' designation.

The Mk 2s were very much more modern in many respects, with less tank-like styling, better handling, lighter interiors and up-to-date dashboards. In addition, they offered better performance, both through increased power in the 2.4-litre engine (which in turn made an automatic transmission option viable) and through the introduction of the latest 3.8-litre engine at the top of the model range. The 3.8-litre Mk 2 was the undoubted star of a revised model range which was rapturously received in all of Jaguar's markets, and for the first few years of the new decade the Mk 2 saloons went on to sell even more strongly than their predecessors had done. Yet their appeal waned quite quickly and with it so did their sales. By the mid-1960s, the Mk 2s were beginning to look old-fashioned, not least against Jaguar's own newer models.

In fact, Jaguar made things very difficult for themselves during the 1960s. The decade started well with the Mk 2s selling strongly, and then in 1961 the company startled the motoring world with two blockbusters in the shape of the sensational E-type (which replaced the XK150) and the astonishingly sophisticated Mk X saloon. The cornerstones of both models were uprated versions of the 3.8-litre engine, plus an ingenious and remarkably refined independent rear suspension. That suspension was so good that it immediately showed up the shortcomings of the cart-sprung, beam-axled Mk 2 saloons and it was not surprising therefore that Jaguar soon started work on what was known internally as a 'Mk 3' compact which incorporated that suspension.

The independent suspension took up very much more room than the old live axle had, and as a result the Jaguar engineers found themselves redesigning the whole of the bodyshell's rear end. This added cost as well as complication, with the inevitable result that the Mk 3 models were going to be markedly more expensive than the Mk 2s. So Sir William Lyons decided that the Mk 3 should not replace the Mk 2 but should be built alongside it as a more expensive companion model, bridging the price gap between the Mk 2 and the big Mk X luxury saloon.

So from 1963 Jaguar's saloon range was swelled by the addition of S-type models, with either 3.4-litre or 3.8-litre engines. Just a year later came another new development in the shape of a 4.2-litre version of the XK engine, which went initially into the Mk X and E-type cars, but it was not long before Jaguar decided to drop it into the S-types as well. This resulted in a further modified car (distinguished by styling changes) called the 420, which arrived in 1966. In the meantime, the Mk 2 compacts were still in production. The net result was that Jaguar's saloon range seemed to be in a constant state of flux in the first half of the 1960s. It must have created all kinds of production headaches at Browns Lane and certainly cannot have made the most cost-effective use of available resources.

These new alternatives from Browns Lane undoubtedly took some of the market away from the Mk 2 compacts, but it was also true that the 1960s had seen the arrival of some exciting new machinery

Figured wood trim and a neat thin-rimmed steering wheel gave the Mk 2 dashboard a very special character. This is a 2.4-litre overdrive model.

which actually made the Mk 2s seem rather old-fashioned. In the competition world (where privateers had continued to uphold the Jaguar sporting tradition), the new Ford Lotus Cortina provided giant-killing performance which left the Jaguars trailing in its wake. Overseas, new models from Mercedes-Benz and others provided attractive alternatives to the Browns Lane cars. And at home, the new breed of executive saloons from Rover, Triumph and others offered many of the Mk 2's qualities and improved on others, all at much lower prices.

THE ACQUISITION OF DAIMLER

Jaguar's complicated model range and the expansion in production which went with it could not have been achieved if the company had not found additional factory space at the beginning of the 1960s: from 18,500 cars in 1959, production was nudging 26,000 by 1964. It was in May 1960 that they bought the ailing Daimler company (together with Guy Motors, Coventry Climax and Henry Meadows) from its BSA owners, who had become disenchanted with its failure to make an impact on the car market during the 1950s. The purchase was intended purely to give them additional factory space, primarily in the Daimler plant at Radford, near Coventry, but Jaguar were not slow to realize the value of the Daimler name as an asset in its own right.

Daimler had not been able to make a success of selling their existing cars and Jaguar were not about to invest time and effort in trying to make them more saleable, although they did make some improvements to the SP250 sports car. They dropped the 3.8-litre Majestic saloon in 1962, as it was in direct (if unsuccessful) competition with their own Mk X, and abandoned the SP250 two years later. As for Daimler's third model, the 4.5-litre V8 Majestic Major, Jaguar kept that in limited production until 1968 because it took them into the limousine market where they had no real presence. From 1968 they replaced it with a new limousine based on the floorpan of the Mk X saloon.

However, Jaguar did pick up Daimler's plans to build a cheaper luxury saloon. Impressed with the 2.5-litre V8 engine which was already used in the SP250 and had been intended for a Daimler saloon which never materialized, they decided to create a new Daimler by using that engine in a Mk 2 Jaguar bodyshell. The result, introduced in 1962 as the Daimler 2.5-litre V8, was a much better car than it had any right to be. And the public accepted it (although exports were as slow as they had been for Daimler in the 1950s), as the activities of BMC and the Rootes Group had already acclimatized them to the concept of badge-engineering. Nor would this be the last 'Daimler-Jaguar': in 1966 the new Jaguar 420 was accompanied by a more luxurious model with Daimler fittings and badges which was known as the Daimler Sovereign, and a similar ploy would be used when the XJ6 arrived in 1968.

MORE MERGERS

The 1960s are sometimes known as the Decade of the Merger, and Jaguar's acquisition of Daimler and its associated companies was certainly not the last merger with which it would be involved. Just a year after the Jaguar move, the Leyland bus and truck company bought out Standard-Triumph, who were suffering a cash-flow crisis caused primarily by a recession in the US car market on which they depended very heavily. Other mergers followed, but in 1965 came the crucial one which would affect Jaguar. BMC, themselves the result of a merger in the early 1950s between the Nuffield Organisation and Austin, bought out the Pressed Steel Company.

This caused ripples of unease throughout the British motor industry. Pressed Steel had been the main independent supplier of body pressings to the smaller car companies, and its ownership by one of the majors put all their futures in jeopardy. For the moment, BMC guaranteed supplies of bodyshells and pressings under existing contracts, but there was no telling what might happen in the future. Sir William Lyons made up his mind quickly: as Jaguar did not have the resources to build its own bodies or to acquire its own body pressings plant, it would have to merge with BMC. Negotiations went ahead with some speed, and during 1966 Jaguar joined forces with BMC in a new alliance known as British Motor Holdings.

This caused further reactions in the industry. Like Jaguar, Rover depended on Pressed Steel for bodyshells and pressings, and they were not slow to see the potential difficulties for them of Jaguar's alliance with BMC and Pressed Steel. So during 1967 they sought shelter in the Leyland group of companies. Meanwhile, the British Government was becoming increasingly anxious about the power of the big multinational car companies like Ford, GM and Chrysler (who all had a stake in the British motor industry) and of the threat which the growth of imported cars presented to the domestic product. In 1968 the Government therefore encouraged British Motor Holdings and Leyland to seek additional strength by combining forces, and a full merger was announced later that year. So it was that within two years, Jaguar passed from an independent company to a member of the British Leyland combine.

ECONOMICS AND EXHAUST EMISSIONS

By the mid-1960s the British economy was in trouble once again. A slump followed the boom years of the late 1950s and early 1960s, and the Government announced an economic freeze in the first half of 1967. The car market was badly affected and Jaguar reacted by making a number of their models cheaper to produce so that they could keep showroom prices down. The final Mk 2 compacts therefore had a number of differences in specification from earlier examples.

By the autumn of 1967 Jaguar had rationalized the position. Partly to disguise the fact that these changes made the cars rather less than they had been, they relaunched the Mk 2s as 240 and 340 models. The 3.8-litre car had gone, thus simplifying the range to save costs and also helping to distance it from the more expensive S-types. The Daimler compact was meanwhile renamed a V8-250, and it took on some of the cosmetic changes associated with the 240 and 340; it was not cheapened in the same way, however, as it generally sold to a clientele which was less affected by the economic difficulties of the time.

Browns Lane had already been working for some time on the car which would eventually replace its compact saloons. In fact

the new car, codenamed XJ6, was scheduled to replace all the existing Jaguar saloons by the end of the decade. One reason for this adoption of a one-model policy had been the announcement in the USA during 1966 that all new cars sold there for the 1968 season would have to meet a set of new criteria. These criteria covered the ability of the car's structure to withstand various types of collision without harm to the occupants, and there were also regulations about protrusions and other items inside the car which could cause injury if its occupants were thrown about in a crash. Then for 1970 there would be further new regulations governing the levels of noxious chemicals permissible in a car's exhaust.

Jaguar soon recognized that the cost of meeting these new regulations was going to be very high indeed. The fact that they had four different saloon bodyshells (Mk 2, S-type, 420 and Mk X) to re-engineer made the potential cost enormous; and the fact that they had five different engines (2.4, 3.4, 3.8 and 4.2-litre XK types, plus the Daimler V8) to adapt for the emissions control regulations simply made the whole exercise too costly to contemplate. What they could afford to do was to make the new XJ6 meet the US safety regulations in time for 1968, and to make one of its two proposed engines (the 4.2-litre XK type and a new 2.8-litre derivative) meet the emissions control regulations by 1970. The way forward, then, was simple. Even though the XJ6 was not a real replacement for the big 420G (née Mk X) or for the Mk 2 compacts, but rather for the middle-range S-types and 420s, it would actually have to replace all the Jaguar saloons. There could be some overlap after its introduction in 1968, when markets outside the USA could take the older Jaguars. But by 1970 they would all have gone.

And so it proved. As far as the original compacts were concerned, the 340 was the first to be withdrawn, in the autumn of 1968. The 240 remained available until the summer of 1969, as did the Daimler V8-250, and in fact the final compact Jaguars to be made were not Jaguars at all but Daimlers. In a production period of fourteen years, a total of 108,850 cars had been built – more than any other Jaguar type until that time, but a far smaller number than Jaguar would achieve with the new XJ6.

Compact Jaguar and Daimler production figures			
Calendar year	Jaguar	Daimler	Total
1955	32		32
1956	8,029		8,029
1957	8,520		8,520
1958	11,605		11,605
1959	11,331		11,331
1960	17,535		17,535
1961	21,236		21,236
1962	12,743	8	12,751
1963	10,253	2,444	12,697
1964	8,074	3,969	12,043
1965	4,847	3,430	8,277
1966	3,735	2,200	5,935
1967	4,662	1,770	6,432
1968	4,626	2,871	7,497
1969	692	1,223	1,915
Total	90,935	17,915	**108,850**

In 1968 appeared the car which was to replace all the Jaguar saloons of the 1960s – the XJ6. The wing mirrors on this very early left-hand-drive example mark it out as one destined for the Swiss market.

3   The First Compact Jaguars

Although many of Jaguar's Engineering records of the 1950s do survive, it is a fact that those relating to the design and development of the compact saloons have disappeared. Perhaps they are still resting somewhere in a dusty filing cabinet, waiting to be discovered some day. Or perhaps – and unfortunately this is far more likely – they were tossed into a skip during the iconoclastic days of Jaguar's ownership by British Leyland. One way or another, the story of the compact saloons' genesis therefore has to be pieced together from the few pieces of the jigsaw which do remain.

THE NEED FOR A THIRD MODEL RANGE

Conventional wisdom insists that Jaguar missed their smaller-engined saloons after the demise of the 1.5-litre and 2.5-litre saloons. The big Mk VII cars with their 3.4-litre engines were selling into the top end of the luxury market, and the would-be Jaguar owner who could not afford a car of that calibre was therefore obliged to turn to another make for his transport. This argument would suggest that Jaguar sales were actually suffering because there was no smaller-engined saloon available after 1950, but sales and production figures show that this was very far from true.

In fact, Jaguar sales had done nothing but increase since the smaller-engined saloons had disappeared. The last 1.5-litre cars had been built in 1949, when Jaguar had built 4,190 cars. The following year, with only 2.5-litre and 3.5-litre engines available in the new Mk V saloons, production shot up to 7,206 cars. Moreover, the best-selling Jaguar of all in 1949 and 1950 was the 3.5-litre engined Mk V saloon; it sold more than three times as many examples as the XK120 sports models and around four times as many as its 2.5-litre companion model. Quite clearly, then, the public was more than happy to accept big-engined Jaguars, and the smaller-engined saloons were not being missed.

So why did William Lyons decide that Jaguar should develop a third range of cars? The answer seems to be bound up with two factors: Lyons' desire to give Jaguar a more solid market base, and Jaguar's expansion in the early 1950s.

Undeniably, Jaguar was doing well as the 1950s began. Sales were up to such an extent that the company was forced to move to the larger premises in Browns Lane simply so that it had enough space to match production to demand. However, there was also no doubt that Jaguar's success was a fragile one. After 1950, with the company dependent on two models selling in specialist market sectors – the Mk VII luxury saloon and the XK120 sports car – its fortunes were heavily dependent on what Lyons would have recognized as volatile areas of the market.

Recent experience had shown that when the economy was in the doldrums, the first sectors of the car market to suffer were precisely those in which Jaguar was operating. There was also the problem that Jaguar were depending more and more on export markets, and events in the early 1950s showed that overseas markets could be closed almost overnight if governments decided to protect their economies by imposing trade bans or high taxation on imports. Jaguar could not risk remaining in this position for long: the company needed a model which would sell in the less volatile middle sector of the market, and one which would sell strongly at home and thus be less dependent on export markets.

Such a car would help protect Jaguar's position against the uncertainties of the world economy, but it would also help the company to continue its expansion if the economic situation remained stable. The new Browns Lane premises were large, and it must have been obvious that Jaguar were unlikely ever to fill them completely with assembly lines for the Mk VII saloons and XK120 sports cars. In order to get the most out of their new investment, therefore, they needed a car which could be made in larger volumes than either of these. If it was successful, it would promote Jaguar from the ranks of the specialist manufacturers into the ranks of the volume car makers, which could only be good for the health of the company. However, it would be important that a new volume-production Jaguar should not debase any of the qualities on which the marque's reputation depended, and it was this consideration which undoubtedly had a profound effect on the eventual design of Jaguar's third range of cars.

DEFINING THE NEW MODEL

Traditionally, sports cars had not been large-volume sellers, and Lyons probably mistrusted the recent success of British roadsters in the USA as something of a flash in the pan: certainly it was a phenomenon which could not be relied upon for the future. The new Jaguar would therefore have to be a saloon, but it could not be an ordinary family saloon because it would be impossible to build a car with Jaguar characteristics at a price which would suit that market. So it would have to be priced to sell on the borderline between the better family saloons and the cheaper luxury models. This was the territory then occupied by makes such as Armstrong-Siddeley, Rover and Riley, and of these only Riley offered a blend of luxury and sporting qualities similar to those associated with Jaguars. As Riley gradually lost their grip on the market after 1950, Lyons must have realized that Jaguar would face very little competition indeed for their new saloon.

So the overriding consideration in designing and developing the new Jaguar must have been price. Starting with an on-sale guide price, Lyons and his advisers must have worked out a maximum production cost after deducting an appropriate percentage for their dealers' and Jaguar's own profit margins. It would have been a complicated set of calculations, affected also by the numbers Jaguar thought they could sell and by the length of time they expected to be able to keep the car in production. At a guess, they probably planned for a ten-year production life (longer than any previous Jaguar or SS car had enjoyed) and this in turn would have demanded that the car should incorporate engineering which would not be outmoded before the end of that projected production life.

The absence of records makes it impossible to be certain when work began on the new Jaguar – codenamed Utah at Browns Lane – but things probably started to get serious some time in 1952. By then, the company had moved into the Browns Lane plant and was able to take a more considered look at the future. By 1952, trade embargos in some overseas markets would have alerted the company to the dangers of relying on two potentially volatile market sectors and on export sales. And, finally, the earliest record of the 2.4-litre engine which was to be the backbone of the new car dates from 1952.

BUILDING BLOCKS

Engines are so expensive to design and develop that motor manufacturers use the same engine in as many different models as possible and Jaguar in the early 1950s were no different from any other car maker in that respect. Besides, their highly-acclaimed twin-ohc XK engine had only entered production in 1948, and was sufficiently advanced to be assured of a lengthy production life. There was therefore no question that the new Jaguar would have a version of the existing production engine.

However, the existing production engine had a capacity of 3.4 litres, and the average engine size in the price bracket where Jaguar hoped to place their new car was rather less than 2.5 litres. The Armstrong-Siddeley engine was a 2.3-litre, Rover had a

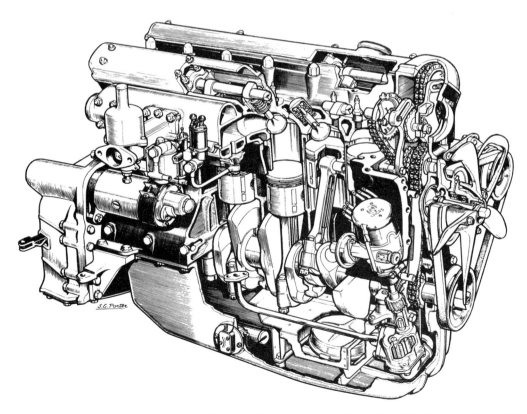

Before work started on the new compact Jaguar, the twin-ohc engine existed in 3.4-litre form. This drawing, originally published in The Motor, *shows an original 1948 example.*

2.1-litre, and the Riley sported the largest engine with 2.5 litres. Power outputs averaged out at a little over 80bhp, with the Riley being by far the most powerful at 100bhp. So it would be reasonable to conclude that Jaguar decided to go for an engine of around 2.5 litres and rather more than 100bhp.

The simplest and cheapest way of developing a smaller-capacity version of the six-cylinder XK engine was to make a short-stroke edition by fitting the 3.4-litre block with a new crankshaft and connecting rods. To produce as near 2.5 litres as possible (in fact, 2,499.69cc), engine number X102 was built with a 77mm stroke and the existing 83mm bore size. It first ran on the test bed at Browns Lane on 25 August 1952, and ended its test cycle some sixteen months later on 11 December 1953.

This first try-out seems to have led to further thoughts; clearly, what the Jaguar engineers called the '2.½-litre six-cylinder engine' was not yet satisfactory. Over the summer of 1953, two further engines went on test, one of them being a refinement of the original 2.5-litre design and the other being a four-cylinder engine of just under two litres' capacity.

The four-cylinder engine, numbered EXP I-1, actually went on test first. Records show that it was first tested on 14 July, but that the test programme was relatively short. The last entry in the engine's test log is dated 10 November 1953, and the idea of a four-cylinder Jaguar engine does not appear to have resurfaced after that.

EXP I-1 had the familiar 83mm bore size and twin-ohc design of the XK engine, but it had a 91mm stroke to give 1,970cc. Running a high 12:1 compression ratio, it initially breathed through two SU HS6 carburettors, which were changed later in the test programme for twin Webers. It was not the first Jaguar-designed four-cylinder and nor was it the only four-cylinder engine

related to the XK design, for Jaguar had originally intended to fit a four-cylinder XK engine into the XK120 sports car to make an XK100 model as early as 1948. However, the company also decided against building this second four-cylinder engine, even though it would easily have produced more than 100bhp and would therefore have met Jaguar's design targets in that area. For on test alongside it was an altogether more promising-looking new variant of the 2½-litre six-cylinder engine.

This new engine had gone on test some six weeks after the four-cylinder, and its first test entry was logged on 26 August 1953. Numbered EXP 2, it had a slightly shorter stroke than the earlier 2½-litre experimental engine to give a swept volume of 2,483cc. Whether it still had a 3.4-litre block or the lowered block eventually adopted for the production engines is not clear; however, it seems quite likely that the new block had been specified along with the shorter stroke.

At this stage, the original 2,499cc engine, X102, was also still on test; but the new engine appears to have proved its worth early on. On 14 October, after less than two months on the test bench, it was joined by a second 2,483cc engine, this one labelled EXP 3. Less than a month later, tests of the four-cylinder engine stopped, and just over a month after that, tests on the long-stroke 2½-litre engine came to an end. The 2,483cc engine had clearly won the day, and by the end of 1953 Jaguar had no doubt settled on this version of the XK engine as the power unit for their new compact saloon.

One further experimental engine of this period deserves mention. This was EXP 9, described as a '2½-litre, light alloy block'. Its test programme started on 1 December 1954, and continued until 3 October 1957. That date provides the clue to what it was, as ten days afterwards Jaguar announced that they would no longer field a works

The XK engine

Jaguar's XK engine was designed to replace the Standard-derived engines on which SS cars of the 1930s had depended. Conceived during the war years, it was developed in 1946–1947 and was ready for production in 1948. Earlier experimental engines included the XF and XG; the name XK was simply the codename applied to the version of the design which Jaguar decided to put into production.

The first car to have it was the XK120 sports model, although this application was really little more than an afterthought; the car for which it had really been intended was the Mk VII saloon which appeared in 1950.

The XK engine was an outstanding power unit, offering exceptional power output and performance. Twin ohcs had been seen earlier in racing engines and in low-volume exotic machinery, but manufacturers had fought shy of using them in volume-production cars because of fears about mechanical reliability and servicing difficulties. The XK engine's greatness lay in the fact that it was reliable, robust, and reasonably easy to work on.

So successful was the design that it remained in production until the mid-1980s. It was made with five different cylinder capacities: 2,483cc (2.4-litre), 2,790cc (2.8-litre), 3,442cc (3.4-litre), 3,781cc (3.8-litre) and 4,235cc (4.2-litre). There was also a special 2,986cc (3-litre) version, used in some of the D-type sports racers. Power outputs ran as high as 265bhp in road-going tune.

The XK engine appeared in the following Jaguar models:

Sports Cars		*Saloons*	
XK120	3.4-litre	Mk VII	3.4-litre
XK140	3.4-litre	Mk VIIM	3.4-litre
XK150	3.4-litre	Mk VIII	3.4-litre
XK150S	3.4-litre	Mk IX	3.8-litre
XK-SS	3.4-litre	Mk X	3.8- and 4.2-litre
E-type	3.8- and 4.2-litre	Mk 1	2.4- and 3.4-litre
		Mk 2	2.4-, 3.4- and 3.8-litre
		240/340	2.4- and 3.4-litre
		S-type	3.4- and 3.8-litre
		420	4.2-litre
		420G	4.2-litre
Sports-racing Cars		XJ6 Ser I	2.8- and 4.2-litre
C-type	3.4-litre	XJ6 Ser 2	3.4- and 4.2-litre
D-type	3.0-, 3.4- and 3.8-litre	XJ6 Ser 3	4.2-litre

In addition, the XK engine was used in several specialist racing cars (notably the Lister) and in the following production vehicles, which all had it in 4.2-litre form:

Daimler Sovereign (badge-engineered Jaguar 420)
Daimler Sovereign (badge-engineered Jaguar XJ6)
Daimler DS420 limousine
Military tracked vehicles   FV101 Scorpion
                             FV102 Striker
                             FV103 Spartan
                             FV104 Samaritan
                             FV105 Sultan
                             FV106 Sampson   (in military form, the XK engine was
                             FV107 Scimitar   known as a Jaguar J60 no. 1 Mark 100B)

competition team. No doubt if the Jaguar works team had continued to exist, sooner or later it would have used cars equipped with the light-alloy engine, and sooner or later the light-alloy engine might have become available in the showrooms. As it was, the project died when Jaguar pulled out of works competition.

While engine development went ahead, some thought must also have been going into other elements of the drivetrain, notably the gearbox. Because the new engine was going to be less powerful and put out less torque than the existing 3.4-litre type, Jaguar would not have to find a stronger gearbox than the one they already had. Automatic transmission was already under development for the Mk VII saloons during 1953 and would be introduced early the following year, but there was no indication that the buyers at whom Jaguar were aiming their new car had the slightest interest in automatic transmission: that was strictly for the luxury market and was in any case not yet popular anywhere outside the USA.

So Jaguar took the simplest and cheapest way out: they decided to use the four-speed Moss gearbox which was already available in both Mk VII and XK120 models. Most probably it was development testing of the completed compact saloon prototypes which showed up the need to alter the second and third gear ratios, but the gearbox selected for production was essentially a familiar Jaguar component. Even the Laycock de Normanville overdrive, which would be offered as an optional extra from the beginning, was identical to that already seen on other Jaguar products.

THE BODYSHELL – STYLING

William Lyons' favoured method of styling a new car was to build a full-size, wooden-framed mock-up and to alter details on that until he was satisfied with the result. Whether he had used this method in the days of SS Cars is not clear, as no pictures are known to survive, but he certainly was using it by the time the Mk V Jaguars were being styled in 1947–8. The Mk VII saloon was styled in the same way and so it was only to be expected that Lyons would use the same proven method for the new smaller Jaguar saloon.

Styling was exclusively Lyons' preserve in the early 1950s. Although he worked with a number of assistants who would modify the panelling of the mock-ups according to his instructions, he had direct and personal control over the finished result: styling was, after all, the skill with which he had made his name in the 1930s. For the new saloon, he started with certain basic parameters which had been agreed with his Chief Engineer, William Heynes – such as the dimensions of the passenger compartment, wheelbase and engine bay – but thereafter the decisions were his.

Several photographs survive of the full-size mock-up for the new small Jaguar saloon, but as they are undated it is impossible to establish for certain the stages through which Lyons' ideas evolved, or even the date when he started work. However, it would be reasonable to assume that the full-size mock-up was put together towards the end of 1952, or some time during 1953, and that the design evolved over a period of several months.

From the beginning, Lyons appears to have been clear that he wanted something different from the sweeping wing-lines which characterized the Mk VII and the XK120. Perhaps one reason was that there already existed a 2.5-litre saloon with sporting pretensions and the sort of sweeping wing-lines which Lyons might have employed, in the shape of the slow-selling Lea-Francis 18hp. Lyons would not have wanted his new Jaguar to look like a revamped Lea-Francis. But a more positive inspiration was undoubtedly the sleek 'pontoon' styling of cars like the 1949 Jensen Interceptor, the 1950 Aston Martin DB2, and the 1953 Riley Pathfinder. Of these, the DB2 in particular seems to have had quite a strong influence on the new small Jaguar.

The Aston, of course, was a two-door sports coupé whereas Lyons wanted a four-door saloon with seating for five. However, it is not hard to recognize the basic shapes of the Aston's lower body and passenger cabin in the Jaguar. Lyons added an XK120-like grille, put the headlamps inboard of the wing ends, added rear spats to give a family resemblance to the XK120 and Mk VII, and hung on some heavy bumpers like those of the Mk VII. On what seem to be the earliest versions of the styling mock-up, there are no panel lines, but one particularly interesting series of later photographs shows panel

lines which make it clear that Lyons was considering a forward-hinged front-wing and bonnet assembly. While it is true that the C-type sports-racing Jaguars had such a feature when they first appeared in 1951, it is also true that the Aston DB2 had a forward-hinged bonnet-and-wing assembly a whole year earlier ...

However, it would be wrong to play down the very considerable skill which Lyons put into styling the new saloon. With the basic shape perhaps conceived as an elongated DB2 with Jaguar styling cues appended, he no doubt began to tinker. And as he tinkered, so the styling model became more and more Jaguar and less and less Aston. The bonnet gained and then lost a raised centre-section; the heavy Mk VII-style bumpers were changed for a much neater and slimmer pattern painted in the body colour, which was sadly rejected; and the grille and sidelights went through a

The 1950 Aston Martin DB2 was probably an influence, conscious or unconscious, on Lyons' styling for the new compact Jaguar.

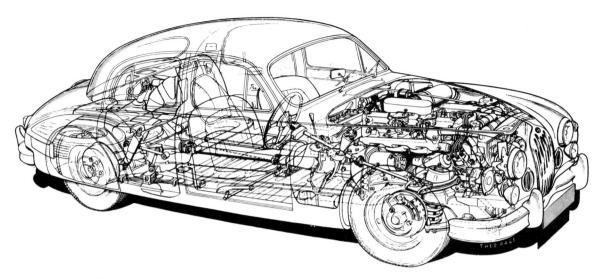

This splendid Theo Page cutaway drawing shows what the 2.4-litre car looked like under its skin.

number of permutations before Lyons was satisfied. Precise dating is problematical, as usual, but it is clear that the basic styling of the new Jaguar had been settled by the early months of 1954.

THE BODYSHELL – STRUCTURE

Lyons and his Chief Engineer, William Heynes, must have decided at a very early stage that the new Jaguar saloon would not have the same body-on-chassis construction as the company's existing products. Among the reasons for this decision was certainly that this traditional method of construction was rapidly losing ground to the newer monocoque structures. The advantages of a monocoque bodyshell might well have been outlined to Jaguar by Pressed Steel, who were already building the bodies for the Mk VII saloons and were no doubt the automatic choice to build bodies for the new saloons too.

In fact, Lyons and Heynes must have recognized that they had little choice. If the monocoque was taking over from body-on-chassis construction, and if Jaguar needed to plan for a long production life in order to make their new saloon viable, there was a very real risk that body-on-chassis construction would appear outmoded before that production life was over. This was something they could not afford to leave to chance. The characteristics of the styling mock-up on which Lyons was working in the early 1950s suggest almost beyond doubt that monocoque construction had been chosen before he started work.

Not the least of the advantages which a monocoque shell offered was that it allowed the car's overall build to be lower because the lowest point of the body did not have to be placed above a chassis frame several inches deep. This suited Lyons' needs admirably, because he wanted his new saloon to have sleek and sporting lines. Monocoque shells could also promise greater rigidity than body-on-chassis construction and this in turn could improve handling by eliminating the flexing to which traditional structures were prone. However, that rigidity could only be achieved by heavy reinforcement of the shell and that brought with it some disadvantages.

The first and most obvious of those disadvantages was a weight increase, which inevitably had an impact on performance. The second disadvantage was that styling sometimes had to be compromised for the sake of strength. This problem was well illustrated from the first, when Lyons' styling mock-up incorporated thick and heavy-looking roof pillars. The production engineers at Pressed Steel seem to have

made those pillars even heavier, with the result that the 2.4-litre Jaguar which went on sale in 1955 lacked much of the grace which Lyons must surely have wished for. It was almost certainly the need for structural strength which put paid to the idea of a forward-hinged bonnet-and-wing assembly too: Pressed Steel must have pointed out that the front of the car would simply have been too weak without rigidly-mounted inner wings, and so the production cars had a conventional crocodile-type bonnet. As time went on and the understanding of structural strength advanced, so monocoque structures imposed fewer restrictions on designers. In the early 1950s, however,

Jaguar played safe with the compact saloon's monocoque. The forward-hinged front wing and bonnet assembly which Lyons appears to have considered was abandoned for a strong box around the engine bay. The inner wings were carefully shaped to cope with the suspension loads. Just visible is the subframe which bore the front suspension assembly.

the universal solution to any doubts about structural strength was to make the suspect component thicker!

There was also a third disadvantage of monocoque structures. Without the benefit of body mountings to insulate the passenger compartment from road noise absorbed by the suspension, they tended to act like a large echo-chamber and amplify every noise which was transmitted through the suspension. Manufacturers had solved this problem with varying degrees of success and Pressed Steel no doubt gave Jaguar the benefit of their experience. However, Jaguar could not afford to make any mistakes in this area, as refinement was one of

the marque's distinguishing characteristics. So it was that Bob Knight was appointed as Development Engineer to take charge of what would nowadays be called NVH (noise, vibration and harshness) work on the new car. The end result was a fine testimony to the thoroughness of a man who, a decade and a half later, would be responsible for making the original Jaguar XJ6 such a supremely refined car.

Structural engineering and styling probably went ahead very much in parallel, with Jaguar's Chief Body Engineer Bill Thornton and his assistant Cyril Crouch doing their best to turn Lyons' styling ideas into metal realities. Production drawings for the

Jaguar had placed the contract for the all-new monocoque bodyshells with Pressed Steel, who produced this ⅜-scale model in transparent plastic in May 1954 to assist in evaluating the design. Details of the structure are quite clearly visible.

The front suspension was mounted on a subframe which incorporated mounting towers for the coil springs. This picture shows the substantial subframe (black) in position under the bodyshell (white). All the early cars, like this one, had drum brakes.

bodyshell were certainly ready by May 1954, because Pressed Steel used them that month to make a three-eighths scale model of the shell in transparent plastic. The aim of this, according to the report they produced later in the year, was 'to reproduce the metal components in sufficient detail (with particular attention to attachment points) to permit of its use in assessing design and production problems as a preliminary to quantity production'. Surviving pictures of the plastic shell suggest that nothing major was changed for production.

SUSPENSION, STEERING AND BRAKES

The essentials of the compact saloon's front suspension were drawn up by William

Heynes. Like the first independent front suspension he had designed for the Mk V Jaguars a few years earlier, it depended on top and bottom wishbones of unequal length. However, where the front suspension of other production Jaguars used the torsion bars which had been inspired by the front suspension of Citroën's 1934 Traction Avant, that of the new car had coil springs. This was one result of the new monocoque construction: finding suitable mounting points for the rear of the torsion bars on the bodyshell proved too complicated.

Whether any prototype cars were built with the front suspension mounted directly to the bodyshell is unclear, but Jaguar certainly decided that this arrangement would not work. The problem was with noise transmission and it was no doubt Bob Knight who recommended using a

From the side, the rear suspension arrangements looked very strange ...

... and they certainly were unusual. This view from below shows how the cantilevered leaf-spring was mounted in a channel under the body and was attached to a bracket on the axle casing. Also visible is the Panhard rod which prevented sideways movement of the axle; its mounting on the bodyshell would always prove troublesome.

The full-size mock-up takes shape. At this stage, slim body-coloured bumpers were envisaged, and the panel-lines behind the front wheelarch suggest that the whole front end would have hinged forwards.

detachable subframe – in effect a miniature chassis – to help insulate the body from the suspension. This subframe was attached to the shell by rubber mountings, soft enough to absorb resonances transmitted to the subframe by the suspension but hard enough to prevent the subframe from moving and so compromising the car's handling.

At the rear, Jaguar initially planned to use conventional semi-elliptic springs, but there were doubts about the stresses which these would impose on the tail of the monocoque: certainly, Rover's experience of mounting springs directly to the rear of the body on their 1948 P3 models had not been a happy one. So instead, Jaguar developed an intriguing cantilevered arrangement, where the axle was mounted to the rear end of inverted semi-elliptic springs, whose front ends were anchored under the rigid central section of the bodyshell. The inspiration for

this arrangement could perhaps be traced back once again to the Citroën Traction Avant, although that car had used torsion bars instead of leaf springs.

At one stage, Jaguar certainly considered providing additional axle location by means of a simple A-frame. This would of course have concentrated a great deal of stress on the point of the A, which would have been fixed to the underside of the body, and the idea might well have been rejected because of fears about the severity of these stresses. Instead, two trailing arms were used, running to separate mounting points on either side of the body; these were complemented by an adjustable Panhard rod which controlled the sideways movement of the axle.

Wheel movement at both front and rear was controlled by hydraulic telescopic dampers, which by the early 1950s had still not completely replaced lever-arm dampers but were generally considered to be more advanced. As there was no reason to deviate from the recirculating-ball steering used in other Jaguars of the early 1950s, the engineers settled on a Burman box for the compact saloons: rack-and-pinion steering systems did exist, but were uncommon and generally gave a heaviness to the steering which Jaguar would not have wanted.

Similarly, although disc brakes did exist in the early 1950s, they remained the preserve of racing machinery and had not yet been developed to the point where they could be used with confidence on a road car. Jaguar therefore settled for drum brakes all round on their new model, although they did make an attempt to overcome the fade which plagued so many other high-performance cars of the period by fitting a vacuum servo. The technology – still quite new on a production car – had been seen before on the Mk VII, but it did not make the compact saloon's brakes totally reliable. Not until disc brakes were ready for production in 1957 could Jaguar be said to have succeeded in that department.

INTERIOR

Jaguar seem to have been determined not to sacrifice interior space in their new saloon, even though the car was to be considerably smaller than a Mk VII and to have a wheelbase which was more than a foot shorter. In developing the interior fittings of the compact saloons, they therefore carved out every bit of space they could, both to create actual passenger space and to create the illusion of space. Rear leg-room was inevitably going to be less than in the Mk VII, but by using thinner front seat backs and shortening both front and rear cushions by 1in (25mm), the interior designers managed to make the passenger compartment appear almost extravagantly spacious. The biggest stumbling block they faced was actually the thick window pillars, which tended to make the interior feel dark and rather claustrophobic.

Certain elements of the design were of course already mapped out by the public's expectations of the Jaguar marque. Even quite mundane family cars still sported leather seat facings in the early 1950s, and so it was automatic that the new Jaguar should do so. Figured wooden trim on the doors and dashboard was also expected of cars in the Jaguar's intended market and so the new saloon had to feature that as well. It has to be said, however, that the design of the facia looked backwards, and was very much in contrast to the forward thinking which was apparent in so many other areas of the car. The main instruments were placed in the centre of the dashboard, which was a deliberate throwback to pre-war fashions; other makers had already adopted more modern layouts with the instruments directly ahead of the driver. Also antiquated was the huge steering wheel with its cone-shaped centre horn push. Much neater types were already on the market, but perhaps Jaguar hoped that their chosen design would appeal to those who remembered the sports cars of the 1930s and now needed to buy a more sensible saloon …

There is one interesting story about the design of that dashboard which bears repeating. William Lyons was a non-smoker and simply did not think of incorporating an ashtray into the wooden dash. However, smoking was distinctly fashionable in the early 1950s, particularly among the sort of people who might be expected to buy the new saloon, and Lyons was eventually persuaded that the car needed an ashtray. To save redesigning the whole dashboard, an ashtray was therefore incorporated below the centre of the dash, concealed behind a wooden fillet. It proved a quick solution to the problem, but also an unsatisfactory one: as the ashtray was directly below the centre-mounted ignition switch, fobs and other keys on the same ring as the ignition key invariably dangled into the open ashtray and spread cigarette ash all over the floor!

PROTOTYPES

Once again, the absence of factory records makes it impossible to establish for certain when the first completed prototypes of the new Jaguar saloon took to the roads. No doubt these cars would have been hand-built examples, as it would have taken Pressed Steel several months to prepare press tools for the new bodyshell and to establish their own production line. Engine test records make clear that at least two prototype cars existed by September 1954, one of them painted grey and the other one painted black. Conceivably, these were the only two prototypes built before the first production car – probably an 'off-tools' proto-type despite its production chassis number – was completed on 7 January 1955.

Pictures do in fact exist of a dark-coloured (almost certainly black) car in an incomplete state. Its hubcaps are painted to match the body (as on the Mk VII), its exhaust pipe emerges from below the centre of the bumper rather than to one side as on production cars, and the details of its rear

lighting and number-plate mounting have clearly not been decided. Quite possibly, this is therefore the first complete prototype of the new saloon.

Other pictures show a light-coloured (possibly grey) car being used for various tests at the MIRA proving ground at Nuneaton, and this car is clearly a proto-type too because its sidelights are off-the-shelf round items which differ from the more consciously styled production type. This car may later have become PVC 302, which Bill Heynes took to France before the public launch; at that stage, it had an inter-mediate style of sidelights, similar to the production type but mounted higher up the front face of the wings. PVC 302 also had Mk VII-style foglights mounted in the wings, but these were not carried over onto production cars, where the recesses in the wings were filled by dummy horn grilles.

As no other pre-production or prototype cars are shown in pictures so far discovered, these two could well be the same two cars mentioned in the engine test records during 1954. If so, perhaps the most remarkable thing about them is that they appear to dif-fer so little from the eventual production cars. Once Lyons had established the styling he wanted on his full-size model, and once the body engineers at Pressed Steel had translated that into a form which could actually be built in quantity, almost nothing changed.

4 The First Compacts, 1955–1959

The first the public saw of the new Jaguar was at the 1955 Earls Court Motor Show in London, which opened on 19 October. Jaguar had stand number 154 on the ground floor of the Exhibition Hall and there they displayed a single example of the new 2.4-litre car alongside a pair of the big Mk VIIM saloons and an XK140 fixed-head coupé. The show car was one of the standard specification models, of which very few appear to have been built: most customers both at home and abroad preferred the 'Special Equipment' model, which for an extra £21 (plus Purchase Tax) came with a very tempting package of extras. The package consisted of a rev counter, a heater, door-operated courtesy lights, vacuum-operated windscreen washers, a rear-seat

The 2.4-litre formed the centrepiece of the Jaguar stand at the 1955 London Motor Show, held at Earls Court. Whitewall tyres were then a fashionable accessory, although it is doubtful whether many of the compact Jaguars had them from new.

arm-rest, a cigar lighter, twin Lucas fog lamps, vitreous enamelled exhaust manifolds and a leaping Jaguar mascot on the car's bonnet.

Nevertheless, enthusiastic would-be owners of the new car had to wait. Production had only barely got under way at Browns Lane, and in fact no more than thirty-two cars would be built before the end of 1955. As a proportion of those had left-hand-drive (the first LHD 2.4 was completed on 21 November) and a further proportion must have been retained at Browns Lane as test and development cars, there can have been very few deliveries to customers in the home market before 1956.

Even the Press had to wait before they

were able to borrow examples of the 2.4-litre Jaguar for road testing, and the two leading British motoring magazines – *The Motor* and *Autocar* – had to wait until the summer before Browns Lane would part with examples. Both were Special Equipment models, registered SWK803 and SWK986 respectively, and both had of course benefited from a number of small improvements which Jaguar had made during the first nine months or so of production. Today, such a long delay between press launch and the availability of press demonstrators would be unthinkable, but in the gentler 1950s the press were rather more forgiving. It was an attitude which allowed manufacturers to sort out initial teething

The rear wheel spats on the original 2.4-litre Jaguar gave it both a family resemblance to the Mk VII and an elegance which later models with cutaway spats never quite equalled. The spats also helped to conceal the narrow rear track.

This rear view of the same car shows how William Lyons and his body engineers had successfully married up the sometimes conflicting requirements of style and structure. The only jarring note is the area behind the rear door window.

problems in a new car without incurring bad publicity, and no doubt Jaguar were grateful for the few months' respite.

PRODUCTION CHANGES, 1955–1957

Considering the amount of new engineering which had been incorporated in the 2.4-litre Jaguar, the car suffered from surprisingly few teething troubles. The service bulletins which Jaguar issued to their dealers reveal that many minor changes were made to the cars' specification, but that few of these were to counter serious faults. Perhaps the worst problem to arise concerned the Panhard rod on the rear axle: a number of breakages were reported to Jaguar, who advised their dealers to weld a reinforcing

plate at the outer end in May 1956, and at the same time introduced an adjustable rod in production which allowed the correct tension to be maintained.

Other problems concerned the rear springs, which could create irritating knocking noises. The first modifications were made in autumn 1956, when a new front mounting plate was fitted to production cars and the spring leaves were given rubber ends. But this was not the whole answer, and further reports of problems came in. Early in 1957 Jaguar advised their dealers to check for distortion of the spring mounting clamps; but even that did not cure the problem completely, and the service bulletins would continue to offer helpful suggestions right through into 1958.

Performance and handling were areas which gave only minor problems. Jaguar decided to fit longer front springs at the end of 1955 to minimize front-end roll, and in the spring of 1956 they made some modifications to the carburettors to deal with complaints about flat spots in low-speed acceleration. The Solex carburettors continued to give occasional cause for concern for the rest of the 2.4's production life, but Jaguar doggedly retained them until 1967. The only other engine changes of note in this early period were in June 1956, when a vibration damper was fitted to the nose of the crankshaft to promote smoother running, and in November that year, when a steel sump replaced the original aluminium type.

Most owners were completely satisfied with the performance of their 2.4-litre Jaguars, although Browns Lane was well aware that there was a substantial minority who wanted more. To cater for them, Jaguar introduced tuning kits during 1956. There were three stages of tune available, all of which made a worthwhile difference to top-end performance but – as Jaguar warned – they did have an adverse effect on acceleration at low speeds. Although these kits were not particularly expensive, they do not seem to have sold in large quantities. Most buyers on the home market probably wanted them for competition purposes and most of the other tuning kits sold probably went overseas to countries where the extra performance would be of greater benefit

Under the bonnet of the original 2.4-litre Jaguar sat the new short-stroke XK engine. The air box on top of the two Solex carburettors was normally fed by a large black air filter box running across the top of the engine; on this example, pictured by The Motor *in 1955, the air box has been turned round and is drawing air through a hose-type duct.*

than on Britain's slow and crowded roads in the pre-motorway era.

The Stage I tuning kit boosted power from the standard 112bhp at 5750rpm to 119bhp at 5800rpm and consisted essentially of modifications to the carburettors and exhaust. Stage II took power up to 131bhp at 5900rpm, and added high-lift camshafts, stronger valve springs and a new distributor to the Stage I modifications. The ultimate was Stage III, which offered 150bhp at 6000rpm, and involved replacing the cylinder head with the new big-valve B-type head as fitted to the 3.4-litre engine in the XK140 sports models. With the new head came twin SU HD6 carburettors and a twin exhaust system. Jaguar also recommended fitting uprated clutch springs to cope with the increased torque of the Stage III conversion.

Gearing came in for early revision too. A 4.55:1 rear axle had been fitted to both overdrive and non-overdrive versions of the original 2.4-litre, but it had clearly proved too low for comfortable cruising with the non-overdrive gearbox. Jaguar countered by standardizing a higher 4.27:1 axle for non-overdrive cars in June 1956 after just 2,188 cars had been built, and at the same time introduced a conversion kit which would allow owners of earlier non-overdrive cars to fit an overdrive. A month later came a further revision, in which a close-ratio gearbox was standardized with the overdrive; non-overdrive models retained the original gearbox.

The cost of these early changes was no doubt absorbed in the price rise of October 1956: from £916 before Purchase Tax, the Special Equipment model soared to £976 before Purchase Tax. However, this was a period of general inflation in new car prices, and the increase was not out of line with the increases made by other manufacturers. A further increase followed in October 1957, when the Special Equipment overdrive car had reached £1,064 (£1,597 7s 0d including

Purchase Tax) from the £1,021 (£1,532 17s 0d) of the previous year. But by this stage, Jaguar had a second compact model on which to concentrate, for the 3.4-litre car had reached the British market.

ENTER THE 3.4

A 3.4-litre edition of the compact Jaguar had been on the cards from a very early stage, and the car's engine bay had been designed to accommodate the 3,442cc engine, which was considerably taller than the short-stroke 2.4-litre type. It seems reasonably certain that the main reason for the car's development was Jaguar's desire to improve sales in the USA.

Well aware that US customers liked both power and automatic transmissions, William Lyons was certainly planning a 3.4-litre Automatic model for that market by autumn 1955, because he refers to it in a letter dated 4 November 1955 to John Dugdale of Jaguar's US subsidiary (reproduced in the latter's book, *Jaguar in America*). At that stage, Lyons hoped that the 3.4-litre model might be ready for March 1956. As things were to turn out, however, the car did not enter production until the beginning of 1957.

There was quite a lot more to the development of the 3.4-litre compact Jaguar than dropping the larger engine into a 2.4-litre bodyshell. The bigger engine demanded an enlarged cooling system and so a larger radiator had to be fitted. To get enough cooling air to that, a larger grille was needed; and to allow for the larger grille, the front wings had to be modified. As the 3.4-litre engine was heavier than the 2.4-litre type, the front suspension had to be beefed up with tougher coil springs. Then a twin-pipe exhaust system proved necessary to allow the engine to give its best.

Next there was the rear axle to attend to,

The 3.4-litre engine was rather taller than the 2.4-litre type, and stood up higher in the engine bay. The SU carburettors and distinctive air cleaner are seen in this picture, which also shows the location of the car's identification plate on the right-hand inner wing.

as the 2.4-litre type was not strong enough to take the vastly increased torque of the bigger engine. In the event, Browns Lane settled for a Salisbury component, using the strong centre section from the big Mk VIII saloon (which already had the 3.4-litre engine) mated to the end sections of the 2.4 compact saloon's axle. Disc brakes were certainly under consideration for the road cars by the time the 3.4 compact saloon was being developed, having already been seen on competition Jaguars, but they were not yet ready for production. So Browns Lane did what it could with drum brakes, and the cutaway rear spats of the production

3.4-litre car were almost certainly designed to improve the flow of cooling air to the rear brake drums and so minimize brake fade. As it was, the early drum-braked 3.4-litre Jaguar was not a car which inspired confidence in high-speed motoring.

By the time the car was ready for production at the beginning of 1957, it had a number of features that distinguished it from the original 2.4-litre model. The cutaway wheel spats and twin exhaust pipes were the most obvious differences, but a closer look revealed the wider grille with 3.4-litre emblem at the top and a chromed 3.4 badge on the boot lid. Like the almost

One reason for the cutaway spats was to allow Jaguar to fit wire wheels with large spinners. Here they are on an early disc-braked 3.4, in this case painted body-colour although they could also be had with silver-enamelled or chrome-plated spokes. This picture shows the dual exhaust pipes which helped to distinguish the larger-engined car.

mythical 'standard' 2.4, the 3.4 had no fog lamps on its front bumper. For the USA and some other export markets, it never would have; but in Britain the fog lamps soon became standard equipment, no doubt in response to customer demand. Most 3.4s were also fitted with the extra-cost option of wire wheels, initially with sixty spokes as on the lighter sports cars, and initially available painted to match the body colour, stove-enamelled in silver, or chromed.

It is interesting that the new car should have been called a 3.4-litre car when it had the same 3,442cc engine as other Jaguars, which had always been known as '3½-litre'

models. Perhaps this was a deliberate ploy to help establish a distinctive identity for the compact model: certainly the analogy of '2.4' and '3.4' made some sense. Whatever the reason, the 3.4-litre engine in the compact saloons came with the same B-type cylinder head, twin SU carburettors and 210bhp power output as it had in the XK140 sports models. That 210bhp gave the car astonishing performance, despite its extra weight as compared to the 2.4-litre models. While a 2.4-litre Jaguar could just about exceed 100mph (160km/h) with a following wind, the 3.4-litre model was capable of 120mph (193km/h). In 1957 that

55

represented very nearly twice the 65mph (105km/h) maximum speed of small family saloons like the Austin A30 or Standard Eight, and had incalculable value in adding to Jaguar's high-performance image.

Automatic transmission versions were not quite as fast as the manual-with-overdrive models, but the losses were mainly in acceleration. For the 3.4 Jaguar had chosen the same Borg Warner type DG box as they had used behind the 3.4-litre engine in their big saloons since 1953. Although American in origin, the box was now being made by Borg Warner at their UK subsidiary in Hertfordshire. It was a three-speed type, complete with full-throttle kickdown, a

solenoid-operated anti-creep device which prevented the rear brakes from being released until the throttle was depressed, and an intermediate speed hold, or lock-up. To save costs, Jaguar had devised an intriguing selector quadrant which was positioned under the centre of the dashboard and suited both RHD and LHD cars. The intermediate-hold switch was separate from the main quadrant, however, and – again to save costs – was fitted into the same hole in the dashboard as was used for the overdrive switch in cars equipped with that type of transmission.

The 3.4-litre saloon was due to go on sale in the USA in March 1957, with UK and

The dashboard of the 3.4-litre car was essentially similar to that of the 2.4 model. This is an early left-hand-drive example with automatic transmission. Note the unusual quadrant selector in the centre of the dash and the intermediate-speed hold switch on the top rail to the driver's left.

other market sales following later in the year, but rumours about its imminent arrival forced Jaguar to acknowledge its existence during February. It was a most inconvenient time: the company was attempting to build up a launch stock for its US dealers so that customers should not have to wait before their orders could be met. Only around two hundred cars – not enough – had been shipped to the USA when the rumours started.

Worse was yet to come. As enthusiastic customers began to make enquiries about the new compact Jaguar, a large area of the Browns Lane factory was destroyed by fire during February. Several examples of the new 3.4-litre car were among those lost in the blaze, but a truly superhuman effort by the Jaguar workforce and by contractors engaged to clear up the mess allowed limited production to restart within nine days and full production to be achieved again after six weeks. Right-hand-drive cars did not become available until May, however, and when *The Motor* magazine asked for a 3.4 to test during April, they had to be content with a left-hand-drive car with automatic transmission (TRW316). As production was still primarily geared to meet demand from the USA, where the car had been ecstatically received, few British customers took delivery before the autumn, by

TRW316 was the 3.4-litre Automatic road-tested by The Motor *for its issue of 10 April 1957. The grille was larger than on the original 2.4 and had a greater number of slats, and there was no doubt that the absence of foglamps tidied up the front end. However, those cutaway spats did show up the narrow rear track, and not always to advantage.*

which time a number of specification changes had already been made.

2.4 AND 3.4 PRODUCTION CHANGES, 1957–1959

Over the next two years, there were dozens of minor changes to the production specification of the 2.4-litre and 3.4-litre Jaguars, but only a very small number of these changes were visible on the surface. The most obvious changes started in September 1957, when Browns Lane saved on production costs and complication by giving the 2.4-litre cars the larger grille of the 3.4-litre models, together with the modified front wings which accompanied it. At about the same time (although the exact date is in dispute), the 2.4-litres also lost their neat rear wheel spats in favour of the cutaway spats fitted to the larger-engined models from the beginning. Then, in November 1957, automatic transmission became available for the 2.4-litre; not surprisingly, the gearbox itself was a version of the Borg Warner DG already available in the 3.4 and in other Jaguars.

Thereafter, visible changes were few and far between. The optional sixty-spoke wire wheels were superseded by a stronger design with seventy-two spokes in January 1959, and at the same time a new knock-on hub-cap (without the protruding spinners of the regular type) was made available with wire wheels for the German market. This was needed to meet new German safety regulations, but Jaguar thought the familiar hub-cap with its twin 'ears' looked better and so the German type never was made available for other markets. Then there were a couple of changes to the interior over the summer of 1958: the original cranked gear lever on manual cars was ousted by a neater-looking remote shift and the illuminated overdrive switch on the dash gave

way to a metal toggle-type switch. No doubt the imminent arrival of the Mk 2 models explains why no visible changes were made in 1959. Nevertheless, there were changes under the skin of the 2.4-litre and 3.4-litre Jaguars until quite late in production.

One problem which had first come to light towards the end of 1956 became a persistent nuisance during 1957 and 1958. Customers complained of knocking noises from the rear of the car, usually most noticeable when the back end was heavily laden. Jaguar were initially convinced that the cause lay in the springs, but the cures they recommended did not eliminate the problem. Then, in September 1957, they decided that the handbrake compensator bracket might be the culprit. Dealers were therefore advised to trim the bracket slightly. However, that was not the whole answer and the problem appears never to have been resolved satisfactorily. No doubt there were actually several different causes of the knocking noises, and no doubt there were also several different varieties of noise: noise types and their apparent locations on a car have always been a subjective issue!

As far as the cars' 'chassis' was concerned, most items were already well-sorted by the time the 3.4-litre models were introduced. There were changes to the dampers in February 1957 and again in November 1958; the front suspension was given progressive bump stops in February 1958 and the free camber of the rear springs was altered that May. In January 1959 came new suspension ball joints with a larger diameter ball and larger angle of movement. The latest Dunlop RS4 tyres replaced the original RS3s on 3.4-litre models built from April 1958, and brought with them better wet-road grip, but the change was never reflected on the smaller-engined cars. Lower-geared steering introduced in April 1959 finally countered the common criticism that the cars' steering was heavy at parking speeds, although it did make for a certain amount of woolliness at higher speeds and did not completely eradicate the problem of heavy steering.

Brakes underwent their most important change in April 1959, when Dunlop's new bridge-type callipers for disc brakes became available and were fitted to all disc-braked models. Their major advantage was that they allowed the friction pads to be changed very easily, without the dismantling necessary with the older disc-brake design. However, smaller changes had been made before that to maintain braking to as high a standard as possible: servos were given an air cleaner in September 1957, and there were modified fixings for the rear calliper adaptor plate from November 1958. Between November 1957 and February 1958, a 5in (125mm) diameter brake servo was fitted in place of the regular 6⅞in (175mm) type on drum-braked cars, although it is not clear whether this was a modification which failed to live up to expectations or simply the result of supply difficulties.

Although disc brakes were so commonly ordered as to be almost standard, drum-braked models were still being made right up to the end of production. The disc brakes were so much better than the drum type, however, that Jaguar introduced conversion kits in January 1958 so that the owners of older drum-braked cars could have their cars' brakes uprated. At the same time, a kit was introduced to allow owners of disc-braked cars to fit wire wheels.

There were several detail electrical changes during this period as well. May 1957 brought a new voltage regulator and July a new wiper motor. Clearly, Jaguar had some misgivings about battery charging because the smaller dynamo pulley fitted from September 1957 made the dynamo run faster and therefore put out more charge at a given engine speed. This suf-

ficed until May 1959, when a larger 25-amp dynamo was standardized.

It is interesting to speculate why Jaguar felt the need for better and better charging systems in their 2.4-litre and 3.4-litre models: there were, after all, very few electrically powered extras to consume the additional current apart from radios and (rarely) supplementary lights. Certainly the 60-watt headlamp bulbs which replaced the original lower-powered type in September 1958 (January 1959 on left-hand-drive cars) and the electric rev counter which replaced the cable-driven type in June 1959 demanded some extra current, but it is tempting to conclude that Jaguar always considered the electrical systems of their early compact models only just adequate for the demands made upon them.

Few changes were made to the transmissions: except for the new gear lever already mentioned, the Moss manual boxes remained unchanged throughout this period. The automatics were modified twice, gaining a more effective anti-creep solenoid in September 1957 and a new valve block (for 3.4-litre cars) in May 1958. Under the bonnet, though, there were many more changes.

The most obvious of these came in May 1957, when the 2.4-litre cars were equipped with the 3.4-style radiator, and then in November 1957 and September 1958 when first the 3.4-litre and then the 2.4-litre models were equipped with oil-bath air filters. Also quite obvious was the twelve-blade cooling fan which replaced the original four-blade type on all engines in November 1958. However, the new fan belt and pulleys fitted to 3.4-litre engines from January 1959 were not immediately visible, and the modified oil filter fitted from July 1957 was well concealed. The invisible changes were to the camshafts in February 1957 (a drilled hole in each cam reduced rattle during a cold start), longer inlet valve guides for the

3.4 engine that September, a new oil pressure relief valve and more durable timing chain dampers in November, and a new thermostat in January 1958. Other changes included carburettor needles for the 3.4 engine in May 1958 and a switch to lead-indium big end bearings on all engines in April 1959.

2.4 AND 3.4 ON SALE, 1955–1959

Production figures show just how successful the compact Jaguars were. Neither the Suez crisis, which blighted the sales of big-engined cars at the tail end of 1956 and during the first few months of 1957, nor the factory fire that destroyed so many

Optional extras for the 2.4-litre and 3.4-litre Jaguars

Alternative tyres (Dunlop Town and Country, Dunlop Fort tubeless, Dunlop Road Speed (for 2.4-litre), Dunlop Weathermaster, Duraband, Goodyear Eagle, India Super, Michelin X radial or whitewall)
Automatic choke cut-out switch for 3.4-litre engines
Automatic transmission
Close-ratio manual gearbox
Competition clutch
Cutaway wheel spats (replacement for full spats on early 2.4-litre cars)
De-mister for rear window
Disc brakes
Disc-brake conversion kit (from early type to later type)
Fire extinguisher
GB letters in chrome for boot lid
Gear lever extension
High-compression (9:1) pistons for 3.4-litre engines
High ratio steering box
Laminated windscreen
Lead bronze engine bearings
Lightened flywheel
Limited-slip differential (Thornton Powr-Lok) for 3.4-litre
Lockable fuel filler cap
Lock set to enable one key to fit all exterior locks
Long-life battery
Master battery switch

Overdrive for manual gearboxes
Passenger grab handle on dashboard
Radiator blind
Radio (several types)
Radio aerial for roof mounting
Radio aerial for wing mounting
Radio aerial for wing mounting (fully retractable by handle inside car)
Radio extension speaker on rear parcel shelf
Rally lamp (by Desmo)
Recalibrated speedometer for use with Michelin X tyres
Rheostat for instrument panel lights
Rimbellishers
Safety belts (front seats only)
Seat adjustment bracket (to raise height of driver's seat by 1in/25mm)
Split bench front seat (automatic type) for manual cars
Steering wheel in white, for export only
Tow-bar (by Witter)
Tuning kits (Stages I to III) for 2.4-litre model
Twin-pipe exhaust system for 2.4-litre models
Uprated anti-roll bar
Uprated headlamps, 40/45-watt Le Mans type
Uprated dampers
Vanity mirror for passenger's sun visor
Wheel trims, Ace Turbo type (to replace standard trims)
Windtone horns (pair)
Wire wheels (body-colour, chrome-plated or silver stove-enamelled)

The 2.4-litre's interior was an interesting mixture of the modern and the traditional. The dashboard with its centrally-placed instruments and the huge steering wheel recalled 1930s practice, and yet the overall ambience was very much more up-to-date. This is a Special Equipment model; the rare standard car had just one large dial in the centre of the dash.

brand-new cars that February, could stop the Jaguars. Production totals for 1957 were marginally better than for 1956 – no doubt helped by the introduction of the 3.4-litre car – and for 1958 they climbed still higher. The 1959 totals, which represented a production period of a little under nine months, were high enough to have achieved a record year if the Mk 2s had not taken over in the autumn.

Although the smaller-engined Jaguar sold rather more in its four seasons of production than the 3.4-litre car in its two and a half seasons, the 3.4-litre was always the bigger seller once the two models were available side by side. Production of the 2.4-litre Jaguar dropped sharply during 1957 and it is clear that the new 3.4-litre

model was taking sales away from the older car. On the home market, however, sales of the two cars were probably fairly evenly matched: the real success of the 3.4-litre car was in overseas markets, such as the USA.

The 2.4-litre Jaguar met with a rather mixed reception when it was launched in the USA in May 1956. While it was undoubtedly a Jaguar to American eyes, it was not the same sort of car as the big Mk VII on which Jaguar's reputation as a maker of luxurious sporting saloons rested. Nor did it have the sort of power which the American market expected. Some of the US dealers actually argued against releasing it in the USA at all, believing that it would be preferable to wait for the 3.4-litre engined car. And certainly, *Road and Track* magazine's characterization of the 2.4-litre Jaguar as a 'compact, safe-handling family car' suggested that they viewed it as rather less of a sports saloon than Jaguar might have liked, even though they were generally enthusiastic about the car and did go on to say that the 'sportscar performance' was 'a bonus feature'.

As John Dugdale reveals in his book, *Jaguar in America,* the company's West Coast office wanted to gather some publicity for the 3.4-litre car by tuning it to run at 150mph (240km/h) across a dried-up lake bed in southern California. However, the cost of preparing the car and the need for direct factory involvement in the project put paid to this idea, and instead the 3.4-litre car was introduced rather more quietly as one of Jaguar's 1957-season models. The Americans did love this car: *Sports Car Illustrated* tested an example in April 1958 and concluded that it was 'a magnificent automobile that no-one in his right mind could seriously fault'. It had performance better than that of American cars with engines twice the size, it had good looks (especially when fitted with wire wheels and whitewall tyres), and it stopped and handled like no other saloon then sold in the USA.

Both in the USA and in other markets, the compact Jaguars and the 3.4-litre models in particular very rapidly acquired the status of coveted possessions. These were cars to respect for their abilities and their good looks, although the rather heavy styling of these early compacts was not universally liked; some people argued that they lacked the feline grace of even the big Mk VII and Mk VIII saloons. In Britain, Jaguars were still viewed in some quarters as a 'cad's car', partly because they were mistrusted as a relatively new make, partly because many people believed real quality could not be had at Jaguar prices, and partly because their high performance image was seen as rather ostentatious. However, this image seems not to have had any significant impact on sales.

2.4 AND 3.4 ON THE ROAD

The 2.4-litre Jaguar was a fast car, four-speed versions giving a maximum speed in the high 90s and more than 100mph (160km/h) being available from overdrive models. That was impressive enough for the mid-1950s; but the 120mph (193km/h) 3.4-litre car's really vigorous acceleration and maximum speed were unmatched by all but a very few cars – and those were much more expensive than the Jaguar and lacked its blend of other qualities.

Jaguar 2.4-litre and 3.4-litre: production figures

Calendar year	2.4-litre	3.4-litre	Total
1955	32		32
1956	8,029		8,029
1957	3,984	4,536	8,520
1958	4,441	7,164	11,605
1959	3,219	5,580	8,799
Total	19,705	17,280	36,985

However, the XK engines gave these cars other qualities too. Their wide torque bands (especially on the larger engine) made them unusually flexible for the time, and ensured that even the giant-killing 3.4-litre car behaved docilely in traffic. Then the care which went into their assembly ensured that operation was smooth right up to maximum crankshaft speeds. The servo-assisted drum brakes provided adequate stopping power for the smaller-engined cars, but the 3.4-litre models really did need the discs which were made optional shortly after production began. Cornering ability was excellent for the times, although the cars' nose-heaviness and rather slow steering meant that drivers needed practice before exploring the limits of that ability. Both 2.4 and 3.4 models were also prone to tail slides when cornering on wet roads, a fault of their narrow rear tracks.

Normally, though, these compact Jaguars were reassuring to drive. They felt extremely solid and their weight made them far less susceptible to cross-winds than some of their contemporaries. They gave a comfortable ride, although their fairly firm seats offered very little lateral support, and they were quiet by the standards of the time even though the tyres did generate quite a lot of road noise. The thick windscreen pillars did give the driver visibility problems at junctions, and the small rear window did not make his task easy when reversing in confined spaces, but contemporary road tests praised the overall visibility from the car, which was good by the standards of the time.

There were few negative features. The steering was very heavy at low speeds, which again made parking a chore. The centrally placed instruments could be hard to read and the long travel of the gear lever on manual-transmission cars was a drawback. The manual boxes also whined quite noticeably in the indirect gears; depending on the driver's point of view, this was either an indication of the age of the gearbox's design, or a pleasant reminder of vintage motoring!

RIVALS

In export markets, Jaguar were not always able to price their compact saloons as aggressively as they might have wished. Import duties, designed to protect domestic products from foreign imports, tended to push prices up. In the UK market, however, where Jaguar could do more or less as they wished with prices, their aggressive pricing strategy was much clearer.

Throughout the second half of the 1950s, the compact Jaguars inhabited a sparsely populated area of the UK car market. They were always very much more expensive than run-of-the-mill family saloons – usually by around 100 per cent – and they were

Jaguar 2.4-litre and 3.4-litre: typical performance figures

	2.4-litre overdrive	3.4-litre automatic
0–60mph	13.5 secs	11.2 secs
0–90mph	38 secs	23 secs
Top speed	104mph (167km/h)	120mph (193km/h)
Fuel consumption	20–23mpg (12–14l/100km)	19–21mpg (13–15l/100km)

also significantly more expensive even than the more upmarket saloons. Nevertheless, they were very much cheaper than the luxury cars of their day.

The buyer with £1,300 to spend who intended to choose his new car from among the exhibits at the 1955 Earls Court Motor Show was not exactly spoiled for choice. If he wanted something faintly old-fashioned, there was the four-cylinder, 1,622cc Lanchester Sprite for £866 plus Purchase Tax (a total of £1,227 19s 0d). For £1,254 17s 6d (£885 plus Purchase Tax), there was the Humber Hawk Estate, a spacious but rather lumbering machine with a 75bhp, 2.3-litre four-cylinder engine. Rather more sporting was the 110bhp, 2.4-litre Riley Pathfinder at £1,240 14s 2d (£875 before Purchase Tax), but it was already beginning to attract a questionable reputation and might not have appeared too attractive.

There were just two six-cylinder cars on offer in this price bracket: the Rover 75 with its 80bhp 2.2-litre engine for £1,297 7s 6d (£915 plus Purchase Tax), and the new compact Jaguar with its 112bhp 2.4-litre engine for £1,298 15s 10d (£916 plus Purchase Tax) in Special Equipment form. The Rover had a far more traditional appeal than the Jaguar and was deliberately aimed at an older and more sedate clientele. For the buyer who wanted performance and refinement, therefore, there was simply no choice: it had to be the Jaguar.

The position changed very little over the next few years. Jaguar did increase the prices of their compact saloons in 1956, but this did not bring them up against serious new competition. The Rover 90 and 105S straddled the Jaguar's price, but the very different appeal of the two marques remained unchanged. The Riley was still cheaper, but its reputation was getting worse. The six-cylinder Humber Super Snipe now entered the equation, but it was once again a large and not very agile car,

while the only newcomer which might have made Browns Lane worry was the Armstrong-Siddeley 236. Buyers soon made it clear that they preferred the Jaguar, however.

Over the next couple of years, Jaguar retained their strong position in this sector of the market. Rover, Riley and Humber remained the main domestic competition and the only other cars in the same price bracket were imports. Cars like the second-series Lancia Appia, the Panhard Dyna, the Citroën DS19, the Simca Chambord and the Studebaker Champion stood very little chance at a time when the British car-buying public had an overwhelmingly patriotic orientation. Likewise, all these cars were designed to sell at lower prices and only came into the Jaguar's price class because of heavy import duties; so they were hardly competitive on specification. In fact, all of them found very few buyers in Britain.

POLICE JAGUARS

No doubt the fact that some twenty British Police forces took 2.4-litre Jaguars on to their strength as patrol cars had a beneficial effect on the cars' public image. In pre-motorway Britain, the extra performance of the 3.4-litre car was probably considered an indulgence, and no 3.4 appears to have been supplied for patrol duties – although some were supplied for plain-clothes work. The majority of the patrol cars were painted black and had tan seats. Mechanically and bodily they were essentially standard production vehicles, but the police specification usually included items such as a calibrated speedometer, a bell and loud-hailer on the front bumper, a radio telephone, an additional rear view mirror for the observer and a variety of lights and signs to meet the requirements of the ordering force.

THE MEXICAN JAGUARS

The prominence of the American, British and continental European markets in Jaguar's sales in the late 1950s tends to obscure the fact that the cars were also sold in other countries, albeit sometimes in only penny numbers. Among the territories for which dealers were appointed was Mexico, and the circumstances of the Mexican market lay behind the establishment of the first – and only – overseas assembly operation for the compacts during the 1950s.

The Mexican Government levied an import tax on all fully assembled cars entering the country from abroad, which made the compact Jaguars unattractively expensive in Mexico. However, Jaguar's importing agent, Mario Padilla, was convinced that he could find a ready market for the compacts if only he could keep the price down – he argued that the way to do this was to assemble the cars in Mexico from kits of parts shipped out by Browns Lane, because locally assembled vehicles were exempt from import tax.

Browns Lane agreed to the idea and after negotiation with the Mexican Government a deal was struck under which the Jaguars would be shipped out to Mexico in semi-knocked-down (SKD) form; in other words, they would be partially assembled at Browns Lane but completed in Mexico. The operation started in August 1957 and ran very successfully until July 1960, when the Mexican Government decided to limit the numbers of motor manufacturers operating in their country and Padilla was obliged to close down his Jaguar assembly lines. In those three years, a total of 214 cars were assembled, 152 of them being 2.4-litres and the remaining 62 being 3.4-litre models. It is interesting to note that the final cars were not assembled until nearly a year after the Mk 2 Jaguar compacts had been introduced in other markets, thus making them probably the last of the original compact Jaguars to be built.

WHAT MIGHT HAVE BEEN

Jaguar were clearly thinking of further developing their compact saloons from quite an early stage and one particularly interesting proposal was a two-door coupé version which was drawn up in 1956. Pressed Steel's body drawings for the car were dated 30 May 1956 and described it simply as a 'Jaguar Sports'. However, there is no trace of a running prototype of the car, and probably the idea for a coupé did not progress beyond the mock-up stage – if indeed the drawings were based on one of Lyons' full-size styling models.

Although the saloon's front end panelling and floorpan would have been retained, the whole of the rear end and the roof panel would have been new, and the two-door body would also have demanded new outer skin panels behind the A-pillar. Perhaps most interesting is that some of the proposed rear-end details anticipated styling solutions seen on the Mk X saloon some five years later.

EPILOGUE

During their production lifetime, the first-generation compact Jaguars were never known by any names other than 2.4-litre and 3.4-litre respectively. However, when the Mk 2 models were announced in 1959, Jaguar themselves began to refer to the earlier models as Mk 1s, and that name has remained in use ever since.

What might have been: this drawing of a proposed 'Jaguar Sports', a coupé based on the 2.4-litre saloon, was prepared by Pressed Steel in May 1956.

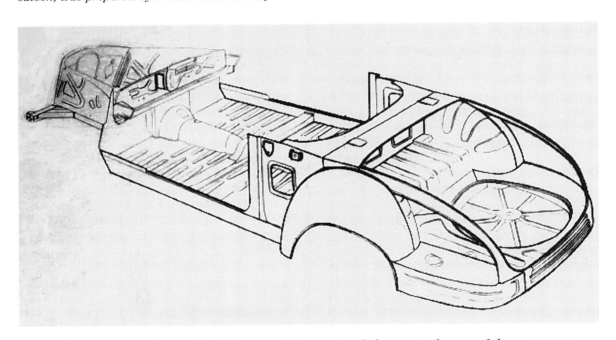

A second drawing from Pressed Steel illustrated the structural changes to the rear of the monocoque. Although it is not clear how far this proposal went, it was certainly serious enough to merit quite detailed work on structural issues.

Identification: Jaguar 2.4-litre and 3.4-litre

Identification numbers are stamped on a plate in the engine compartment, attached to the right-hand inner wing. The engine number, body number and gearbox number are repeated elsewhere as shown below.

Car (chassis, VIN) number

The Car Number is found only on the plate on the right-hand inner wing. A typical Car Number would be 905302DN. This breaks down into three elements:

90	model type code (some had three digits; see below)
5302	serial number (see below)
DN	transmission type (see below)

Sequences are as follows:

	RHD	LHD
2.4	900001 – 916250	940001 – 943742
3.4	970001 – 978945	985001 – 993461

Suffixes are:

BW	Borg Warner automatic gearbox
DN	(Laycock) DeNormanville overdrive

Engine Number

The Engine Number is stamped on the right-hand side of the cylinder block above the oil filter and again at the front of the cylinder head casting, beside the front spark plug hole. A typical engine number would be BC3501/8. This breaks down into three elements:

BC	engine type identifier (see below)
3501	serial number (see below)
/8	compression ratio (see below)

Sequences are as follows:

2.4	BB, BC, BD, BE
3.4	KE, KF

Suffixes are:

/8	8:1 compression ratio
/9	9:1 compression ratio

Body Number

The body number is stamped on a small plate attached to the right-hand side of the scuttle, under the bonnet. It generally has four digits.

Gearbox Number

The gearbox number of manual and overdrive gearboxes is stamped on a small shoulder at the left-hand rear corner of the gearbox and on the rim of the core plug aperture on the top cover. The gearbox number on cars with automatic transmission is stamped on a plate attached to the left-hand side of the transmission casing.

2.4-Litre (1955–1959)
Layout
Monocoque bodyshell with front subframe bolted in place. Five-seater saloon, with front engine and rear wheel drive.

Engine

Type	XK, twin overhead camshaft
Block material	Cast iron
Head material	Aluminium alloy
Cylinders	Six, in line
Cooling	Water
Bore and stroke	83mm × 76.5mm
Capacity	2,483cc
Main bearings	Seven
Valves	Two per cylinder
Compression ratio	8:1 (7:1 optional)
Carburettors	Twin Solex B32-PBI-5 (twin SU optional)
Max. power	112bhp @ 5,750rpm
Max. torque	140lb/ft @ 2,000rpm

Tranmission

Manual models	Hydraulically operated single dry plate clutch, 9in diameter
Automatic models	Torque converter

Internal gearbox ratios

Option 1   Four-speed manual

Top	1.00:1
Third	1.36:1
Second	1.98:1
First	3.37:1
Final drive	4.55:1

Option 2   Four-speed manual with overdrive

Overdrive	0.77:1
Top	1.00:1
Third	1.36:1
Second	1.98:1
First	3.37:1
Final drive	4.27:1

Option 3   Three-speed automatic

Top	1.00:1
Intermediate	3.09:1
First	4.97:1
Final drive	3.54:1

Suspension and steering

Front	Independent, with wishbones, coil springs and anti-roll bar
Rear	Live axle with radius arms, Panhard rod and semi-elliptic leaf springs
Steering	Recirculating ball, worm-and-nut
Tyres	6.40 × 15 crossply
Wheels	Five-stud disc type; optional wire-spoke type
Rim width	4.5in

Brakes

Type	Servo-assisted drums font and rear (discs optional from late 1957)
Size	Drum diameter 11.125in; disc diameter 12in

Dimensions (in/mm)

Track, front	54.625/1,387
Track, rear	50.125/1,273
Wheelbase	107.375/2,727
Overall length	180.75/4,591
Overall width	66.75/1,695
Overall height	57.5/1,460

Jaguar 3.4-litre (1957–1959)

Layout

Monocoque bodyshell with front subframe bolted in place. Five-seater saloon, with front engine and rear wheel drive.

Engine

Type	XK, twin overhead camshaft
Block material	Cast iron
Head material	Aluminium alloy
Cylinders	Six, in line
Cooling	Water
Bore and stroke	83 × 106mm
Capacity	3,442cc
Main bearings	Seven
Valves	Two per cylinder
Compression ratio	8:1 (7:1 and 9:1 optional)
Carburettors	Twin SU HD6
Max. power	210bhp @ 5,500rpm (with 8:1 compression)
Max. torque	216lb/ft @ 3,000rpm

Transmission

Manual models	Hydraulically operated single dry plate clutch, 9in diameter
Automatic models	Torque converter

Internal gearbox ratios

Option 1 Four-speed manual

Top	1.00:1
Third	1.28:1
Second	1.86:1
First	3.37:1
Final drive	3.54:1

Option 2 Four-speed manual with overdrive

Overdrive	0.77:1
Top	1.00:1
Third	1.28:1
Second	1.86:1
First	3.37:1
Final drive	3.77:1

Option 3 Four-speed close-ratio manual

Top	1.00:1
Third	1.21:1
Seconds	1.36:1
First	2.98:1
Final Drive	3.54:1

Option 4 Three-speed automatic

Top	1.00:1
Intermediate	3.09:1
First	4.97:1
Final drive	3.54:1

Suspension and steering

Front	Independent, with wishbones, coil springs and anti-roll bar
Rear	Live axle with radius arms, Panhard rod and semi-elliptic leaf springs
Steering	Recirculating ball, worm-and-nut
Tyres	6.40 × 15 crossply
Wheels	Five-stud disc type; optional wire-spoke type
Rim Width	4.5in

Brakes

Type	Servo-assisted drums front and rear (discs optional from late 1957)
Size	Drum diameter 11.125in; disc diameter 12in

Dimensions (in/mm)

Track, front	54.625/1,387
Track, rear	50.125/1,273
Wheelbase	107.375/2,727
Overall length	180.75/4,591
Overall width	66.75/1,695
Overall height	57.5/1,460
Unladen weight	3,192 lb/1,448kg

Colours and trims – Jaguar 2.4 and 3.4 models

Throughout the production run of the 2.4-litre and 3.4-litre compact saloons, Jaguar were prepared to supply cars painted and trimmed to special order, and several such cars were in fact supplied.

September 1955 to March 1956
There were ten standard paint colours with six interior trim colour options:

Battleship Grey	with trim in	Grey or Red
Birch Grey		Grey, Pale Blue or Red
Black		Biscuit, Grey, Red or Tan
British Racing Green		Green or Tan
Dove Grey		Biscuit or Tan
Lavender Grey		Green or Red
Old English White		Red
Pastel Blue		Blue or Grey
Pastel Green		Green
Suede Green		Green

April 1956 to December 1956
There were thirteen standard paint colours with six interior trim colour options:

Battleship Grey	with trim in	Grey or Red
Birch Grey		Grey, Pale Blue or Red
Black		Biscuit, Grey, Red or Tan
British Racing Green		Green or Tan
Carmine Red		Red
Dove Grey		Biscuit or Tan
Lavender Grey		Green or Red
Maroon		Biscuit or Red
Old English White		Red
Pastel Blue		Blue or Grey
Pastel Green		Green
Pearl Grey		Blue, Grey or Red
Suede Green		Green

January 1957 to October 1957

There were seventeen standard paint colours with six interior trim colour options:

Battleship Grey	with trim in	Grey or Red
Birch Grey		Grey, Pale Blue or Red
Black		Biscuit, Grey, Red or Tan
British Racing Green		Green or Tan
Carmine Red		Red
Claret		Red or Tan
Cotswold Blue		Blue or Grey
Dove Grey		Biscuit or Tan
Imperial Maroon		Biscuit or Red
Indigo Blue		Blue or Grey
Lavender Grey		Green or Red
Old English White		Red
Pastel Blue		Blue or Grey
Pastel Green		Green
Pearl Grey		Blue, Grey or Red
Sherwood Green		Green
Suede Green		Green

November 1957 to December 1957

There were fourteen standard paint colours with six interior trim colour options:

Black	with trim in	Biscuit, Grey, Red or Tan
British Racing Green		Green or Tan
Carmine Red		Red
Claret		Red or Tan
Cotswold Blue		Blue or Grey
Dove Grey		Biscuit or Tan
Imperial Maroon		Biscuit or Red
Indigo Blue		Blue or Grey
Lavender Grey		Green or Red
Old English White		Red
Pastel Green		Green
Pearl Grey		Blue, Grey or Red
Sherwood Green		Green
Suede Green		Green

January 1958 to (probably March) 1959

There were fourteen standard paint colours with six interior trim colour options:

Black	with trim in	Biscuit, Grey, Red or Tan
British Racing Green		Green or Tan
Carmine Red		Red
Claret		Red or Tan
Cotswold Blue		Blue or Grey
Dove Grey		Biscuit or Tan
Forest Green		Green or Grey
Imperial Maroon		Biscuit or Red
Indigo Blue		Blue or Grey
Lavender Grey		Green or Red
Old English White		Red
Pastel Green		Green
Pearl Grey		Blue, Grey or Red
Suede Green		Green

(Probably March) 1959 to September 1959

There were eight standard paint colours with six interior trim colour options:

Black	with trim in	Biscuit, Grey, Red or Tan
British Racing Green		Green or Tan
Carmine Red		Red
Cotswold Blue		Blue or Grey
Imperial Maroon		Biscuit or Red
Indigo Blue		Blue or Grey
Old English White		Red
Pearl Grey		Blue, Grey or Red

Note: Pearl Grey existed in at least three slightly different shades between 1956 and 1959.

5 Development of the Mk 2

It is difficult to establish from surviving records exactly when the focus of development work on Jaguar's compact saloons switched from improving the existing cars to preparing the car which would go on sale in October 1959 as the Mk 2. However, the late Jaguar historian Andrew Whyte believed that the Utah facelift or Utah Mk 2 took shape over the summer of 1958.

By this time, the original cars had been around long enough for a convincing volume of customer feedback to make clear what Jaguar had to do next. The question of a power increase had already been addressed with the 3.4-litre model, but there had been other criticisms too: outmoded and bloated styling, tricky high-speed handling, old-fashioned interior design, inadequate heating and ventilation, and poor driver visibility. These, then, were the areas which the

This low-angle shot shows some of the key features of the Mk 2. The sidelights moved to the wing tops, leaving room for indicators in the front wings, and foglamps were fitted in place of the dummy horn grilles on the earlier cars. The overriders were also moved outwards to make the car look wider. This example is wearing the optional Ace Turbo wheel trims.

Jaguar engineers now started to address.

Resources were not limitless, of course. Rebuilding operations after the disastrous Browns Lane fire of February 1957 must have consumed some of Jaguar's capital, even though the bulk of the £3.5 million damage caused would have been reclaimed from the company's insurers. It was also true that making major changes – for example, to the bodyshell – was bound to be very expensive indeed. As the car had been on sale for only a few years, the cost of the original press tools had still not been amortized, and it would clearly have been wasteful to make massive changes.

Exactly what Sir William Lyons instructed his development engineers to do is not clear, but his brief was probably that they should make the car look as fresh as possible and address all its mechanical shortcomings while making the minimum possible number of alterations. In addition, it looks as if they were asked to give the car more luxury features. It must have been a difficult task, but the Browns Lane engineers rose to it magnificently.

STYLING

No doubt the major alterations to the look of the car were carried out under the close supervision of Sir William Lyons and no doubt various solutions would have been tried out on a full-size bodyshell or mock-up shell. The inner structure of the existing bodyshell was retained intact, primarily no doubt to reduce cost and complication, and all the alterations were made to the outer skin. Even so, some of these modifications did affect the basic structure of the car, because of course the roof panel was a stressed component integral to the monocoque.

It was in the area of the passenger cabin that the most radical styling alterations

One of the clumsiest elements of the original compact Jaguars had been the area around the rear-window pillars. For the Mk 2 models, larger rear quarter-lights both tidied up the exterior styling and brought welcome extra light into the rear seat area. Chromed window frames also helped to give the car a more graceful appearance. Note also the new style of door handles designed for the Mk 2 models.

were made. Out went the heavy window pillars of the original car, probably included at the insistence of nervous stress engineers who wanted to build the maximum possible strength into the monocoque. In their place came a much larger glass area (allegedly developed at MIRA), which looked even more generous than it was because the side window frames were chromium plated. A

The grille was given additional character for the Mk 2 models by a prominent vertical bar. It is seen here on a 1967 340 model, the successor to the 3.4-litre Mk 2.

key element in this was the rounded rear quarter-light which reached back into the rear roof pillar; in shape, it cleverly evoked the lines of the big Jaguar saloons (by now Mk VIIIs and soon to become Mk IXs), and thus created a welcome family resemblance. No doubt Sir William was pleased to have the opportunity to re-use a most successful Jaguar styling trademark which dated from at least ten years earlier.

The roof panel, too, was altered. It was made slightly flatter than before and its apparent height above the door openings was lessened by chromed rain gutters which ran right around the new line of the windows. At the front, 1in (25mm) added to the depth of the windscreen ate into the metal of the roof, while there were also considerable changes at the rear. Here, a semi-wrap-around window was fitted, 7in

(178mm) wider than the earlier type and also 3in (76mm) deeper.

These modifications required only minimal alterations to the body tooling held by Pressed Steel and yet their overall effect was nothing short of astonishing. From all angles, the car looked lighter and slimmer than before and yet the basic lines remained familiar. It might not be fanciful to suggest that the transformation wrought here was one of the most masterful ever achieved in the history of Jaguar; certainly it was extraordinarily successful and it made the car look more modern as well as prettier.

Below the waistline, the basic shape of the car was not changed, although there were several differences of detail. The lower door panels retained their existing profiles and the only modification here was to their exterior handles, now more curvaceous and less 'antique' in style (and also less prone to freezing up in cold weather, which was one of their design aims). The rear wing panels and rear valance did have to change in order to accommodate engineering changes underneath, but they looked very much the same as before. The rear wheel spats, too, retained their basic shape – although a subtle change at their trailing edges gave them a rather happier appearance.

Also subtle were the changes to the rear bumper, which was actually wider than before to accommodate changes under the skin of the car, but looked very much the same. It did not take sharp eyes to spot one important difference, however, for the bumper now displayed a circular emblem which warned following drivers that this car had disc brakes – and was therefore likely to stop rather more quickly than they

might be able to! While they were working on the rear, Jaguar had also managed to turn the rather untidy-looking exhaust tailpipe into a proper styling feature: the exhaust now terminated in a business-like twin outlet on the left-hand side of the car, just below the valance. To complete the picture, there were new and larger rear lamp clusters, similar in concept to those on other models and thus reinforcing the family connection – although, as so often with Jaguars, they were not identical to those fitted to any other model!

More changes were made at the front, however. While the basic styling of the wings was unchanged, the panels were modified to accommodate new lighting arrangements. Sidelights were fitted in pods on the wing crowns to enhance the family resemblance to other Jaguar models and new circular indicator lamps were

New tail-lamp clusters were also designed for the Mk 2. Although they were generally similar to those on other Jaguar models of the time, they were in fact unique. This example is seen on a later 340 model.

The Mk 2 sidelights were designed with a useful translucent plastic 'tell-tale', which reassured the driver that the light was actually working. On the very first cars, they were in white plastic, but most Mk 2s had them in red like this one.

added to the wing fronts. The horn grilles were replaced by fog lamps which fitted neatly into the recesses, Mk VII-style, and thus prevented the sometimes untidy-looking front ends created when owners added free-standing lamps to the earlier cars. Last but not least, the overriders were moved outwards to make the car look wider, and a new grille with prominent vertical bar was added.

INTERIOR CHANGES

There had been little to criticize about the interior of the original compact Jaguars beyond the anachronistic dashboard layout and huge four-spoke steering wheel. By the end of the 1950s, vintage touches such as these – which did have a certain appeal back in 1955 – had become a liability, and Jaguar resolved to change them. However, the redesign for the Mk 2 cars did not stop there. Customers seemed to want the compact Jaguars to incorporate the luxury features fitted to the big saloons as well, and so Browns Lane restyled not only the dashboard but also the seats and door trims. The restyle was so extensive that very little of the original interior design was left in the end.

The first thing to do was to move the instruments from the centre of the dashboard to a position directly ahead of the driver. This made the provision of right-hand-drive and left-hand-drive versions slightly more complicated than before, but it did result in a dashboard which was very much more modern-looking than before, as well as much easier to use. The wooden panel containing the two major dials – speedometer and rev counter – was matched in size by a passenger-side panel which incorporated a lockable glove-box with drop-down lid, and by careful arrangement of the surrounding panels Jaguar were able to minimize the number of different dashboard panels they had to manufacture.

This much was relatively straightforward, and successfully retained the traditional wooden-dash appeal which Jaguar customers so loved. However, the real master-strokes in the redesign resulted from a decision to incorporate a more modern-looking steering wheel and a black-finished centre panel containing the auxiliary instruments and switchgear. The old four-spoke wheel which would not have looked out of place on a vintage Bentley was replaced by a neat two-spoke type in black plastic, set off by a chromed half-ring to operate the horn. And in the centre of the facia, the row of four auxiliary instruments flanking the main lighting control and sitting above six toggle switches (all neatly labelled) together with the ignition keylock and starter switch created a classic layout which was carried over in its essentials to the XJ6 of 1968. In use, it was not particularly good, but it certainly looked the part!

The redesign did not stop there. Recognizing that more and more customers were now ordering car radios, Jaguar designed a neat downward extension of the facia, which met up with a centre console between the front seats and incorporated space for a radio and its speaker. The heating and ventilation controls were neatly arranged on either side and a large ashtray was fitted into the horizontal surface of the console ahead of the gear lever. This new arrangement left no room for the awkward selector lever on cars with automatic transmission (on a quadrant under the dash centre), and so the selector was repositioned much more sensibly on the steering column. A window in the top of the column shroud provided visual indication of the transmission mode selected, and this same window was employed on manual cars with different lettering behind it: on four-speed cars, it simply read 'Jaguar', and on overdrive models, it read 'Overdrive' and lit up when the overdrive was engaged.

Dark walnut veneer was chosen for the dashboard and of course was also used on the obligatory wooden door cappings. Below these, the door trims were also completely redesigned, with new arm-rests and new fluting to give a less spartan look than the originals. The rear seat remained substantially unchanged (although its top panel was now made of a single piece of leather instead of two pieces joined in the middle), but the front seats were quite radically altered. Fitted with wider cushions and deeper squabs, they looked more luxurious than the earlier type, although in practice they provided less lateral support and were not as well suited to a sports saloon. In keeping with the greater emphasis on luxury fittings, they also had fold-down veneered picnic tables in their backs which matched the rest of the wood inside the car.

MECHANICAL CHANGES

As one of Jaguar's strong suits had always been strong performance supported by first-rate handling and braking, the criticisms of the latter two levelled at the early compact saloons must have hurt. As Chapter 4 makes clear, several running alterations were made to the original cars to improve things: disc brakes and modified front suspension among them. However, there was little doubt that the biggest obstacle to better handling lay in the original narrow-track rear axle. At moderate speeds, it could make the car feel disconcertingly unresponsive through a series of S-bends, while at higher speeds it was responsible for a certain amount of instability. Clearly, the revised compact Jaguars had to offer improvements in this important area.

During the late 1950s the Browns Lane engineers were working on a new independent rear suspension which would make its debut in the 1961 Mk X saloon and E-type sports car. However, there was no chance that this would be ready in time for the revised compact saloons – and even if it had been, it is questionable whether Jaguar would have wanted at this stage to spend the money necessary to redevelop the bodyshell to take it. So the solution to the compact saloon's handling problems had to be a compromise and in fact the engineers found that by simply fitting a wider rear axle and retaining the existing suspension, the car's handling was greatly improved. It was this wider axle – which set the rear wheels 3.25in (82mm) further apart – which made necessary the rear end panel changes already outlined.

Not content with that, Browns Lane also modified the front suspension. The aim here was to reduce roll in corners, and this was achieved by placing the pivots of the upper and lower wishbones slightly further apart and by angling both wishbones downwards. The effect was to raise the roll centre of the car. In tandem with the new rear axle, the modified front suspension made for a car which remained more level and more controllable in corners, while also being less twitchy at high speeds.

All this ironed out the basic problems, and of course stopping was well catered for by the all-round disc brakes which had been standard since January 1959. Steering, too, needed no major attention – although there had been well-founded criticisms that it was unacceptably heavy at low speeds. Anxious to counter this, and also anxious to offer a power-assisted option for the American market where such things were more or less taken for granted, Jaguar turned to Burman, who had provided the box available on the Mk VIII saloon after April 1958, and to Hobourn-Eaton, who had provided the engine-driven hydraulic pump.

The installation eventually chosen for the Mk 2 was different in many respects from that in the big saloons – not the least of them being that the steering box was rather smaller to suit the space available. Once again, however, it was clear that a great deal of care had been taken to minimize the cost of the installation. The Burman box bolted directly to the same front subframe as was used in compact saloons without power steering, and the only change which went with it was a pair of tougher steering arms which would resist damage if the wheels were turned against an obstruction, such as a kerb.

It is rare indeed that later developments of an original design end up losing weight, and the Mk 2 Jaguars were no exception. In final production form, they were 112–167lb (51–76kg) heavier than their predecessors, an increase which must have been clear quite early on during the development stages. As weight is one of the biggest enemies of performance, clearly more powerful engines were going to be needed.

The increased weight certainly did make a difference to the 2.4-litre model, and the simple solution – at least on paper – seemed to be to fit the big-valve B-type cylinder head to the 2.4-litre engine. The results were 120bhp as against 112bhp in the original car, and 144lb/ft of torque as against 140lb/ft. This sounded as if it would do the trick, but in practice it fell far short of what was needed. Jaguar were dismayed to find out too late that their calculations were wrong and that the 2.4-litre Mk 2 was markedly slower than the original car – it would not even reach 100mph (160km/h) flat out! Not surprisingly, the factory never allowed examples of the 2.4-litre Mk 2 to be road-tested by motoring journals which took accurate performance figures …

As for the 3.4-litre engine, its 210bhp was enough to maintain the performance of the original 3.4-litre cars in the heavier bodyshell without difficulty. However, Jaguar were well aware that there was a demand for even greater performance, both from drivers who used their compact saloons for competitions work and from certain overseas markets, notably the USA. They therefore decided that there would be a third and even more powerful Mk 2 compact saloon, this one using the 3.8-litre version of the XK engine which was the largest then available to Jaguar.

The 3.8-litre engine was first announced in 1958 for the XK150 sports cars and for the Mk VIII saloons. It was essentially a large-bore version of the 3.4-litre type, and offered substantial increases in both power and torque over the smaller engine. For the Mk 2 Jaguar, it was used in 220bhp, twin-carburettor, Mk IX tune. As the external dimensions of the two cylinder blocks were identical, installation of a 3.8-litre engine in an engine bay designed to accept the 3.4-litre type presented no problems and probably relatively little development

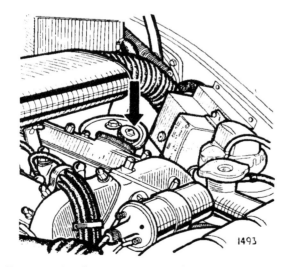

Power-assisted steering was an important addition for the Mk 2 models. Jaguar had little choice about where to put the fluid reservoir in an already crowded engine bay, but found room for it above the exhaust manifold.

work was necessary. However, it did become clear during development that the massive torque of the 3.8-litre engine would very easily provoke wheelspin in the compact Jaguar and so a Powr-Lok limited-slip differential was specified as standard equipment on production cars. The Powr-Lok had actually been designed by the Thornton Axle Company in the USA, but the version Jaguar used was built under licence in Britain.

PROTOTYPES

Strangely, rather less information has survived about the Mk 2 prototypes than has survived about the earlier Mk 1 prototypes. Dates, too, are problematical but no doubt 1958 would have been the key year in Mk 2 development.

The initial Mk 2 prototypes were simply modified Mk 1 cars, and among them was a black 3.4-litre known at Browns Lane as the 'wide-track car' which was used for development of the Mk 2's wider rear axle. The same car was fitted experimentally in July 1959 with Lucas petrol injection in place of its twin SU carburettors, but nothing came of these experiments as far as the Mk 2 was concerned. The 3.8-litre Mk 2 was also developed on a Mk 1 'mule', this one a Sherwood Green 3.4-litre, registered TVC 420. Its new engine (number NC4243/8) was a modified production 3.8-litre type which was fitted as late as 4 June 1959 – just a few months before the 3.8-litre Mk 2 was announced.

Once the major modifications to the Mk 1 compacts had been thoroughly tested on development prototypes like these, Jaguar probably built a small run of off-tools prototypes. These would have been assembled by hand, using the production components, to check for assembly problems. Production records suggest (but do not confirm) that these off-tools prototypes were actually built during August, September and October 1959 – only just in time for the Mk 2's public launch to be followed by volume production.

6 The Mk 2 in Production

Perhaps the neatest summary of what made the Mk 2 Jaguar so special was provided by Jim Randle, then the company's Chief Engineer, during the 1986 launch of the new XJ40 saloon. In his words, 'an outstandingly beautiful car, it clearly established the company's position as a class leader in terms of value for money, performance, state-of-the-art handling, high-quality interior appointments and distinctive exterior styling'. No one who has had any experience of the Mk 2 is likely to disagree with that.

The very first Mk 2 to be built appears to have been a right-hand-drive 3.4-litre car, completed on 15 July 1959. The first 2.4-litre car followed in August. However, these were isolated examples which must have been used to test build methods. Volume production of Mk 2s began in September with left-hand-drive 3.8s for the US market that was so important to Jaguar; right-hand-drive 2.4s and 3.4s followed in October, and right-hand-drive 3.8s were the last to arrive, during November.

The launch announcement of the Mk 2 models was made on 2 October 1959, just under three weeks before the Earls Court Motor Show which would be the new model's first public airing. This allowed the press to publish their initial reports and

The Mk 2 Jaguar took pride of place on the Jaguar stand at the 1959 London Motor Show. The wire wheels and whitewall tyres seen on this 3.4-litre model were of course optional extras. In the foreground is one of the old-model 2.4-litre cars which would tide dealers over until the Mk 2s became available in quantity.

thus to whet the appetites of potential Mk 2 customers. However, cars were simply not available in most markets before the end of November or beginning of December, as volume production had not yet begun. Even in the USA, where initial production of the 3.8-litre models was used to build up dealer stocks before the launch announcement, no cars were available before the end of October.

Elsewhere, the customers had to wait. The original 2.4-litre and 3.4-litre saloons remained on sale and what Jaguar now called a 'standard' 2.4-litre car was on the Earls Court stand alongside examples of the 2.4-litre and 3.4-litre Mk 2s. The run-out stocks of these earlier cars were available only with what had earlier been the Special Equipment specification, and tided Jaguar's dealers over until the Mk 2 models became available in quantity. Any

A comprehensive tool kit was always part of the Mk 2 specification. It was fitted in its own casing and was stowed in the centre of the spare wheel well.

Mk 1s which remained in the showrooms after the end of the year must have been difficult to sell: the Mk 2s offered so many advantages for a price increase of around 6 per cent that few buyers can have been tempted by the cheaper old models.

It was the British magazine *Autocar* that published the first road test of a Mk 2 Jaguar, at the end of February 1960. Not surprisingly, Jaguar had offered them a 3.8-litre model with overdrive; equally unsurprisingly, the magazine's testers were enthusiastic about the car. Their enthusiasm was carefully reined in in that characteristically British manner, however, and it was certainly not untempered by criticisms. *Autocar* praised the car's performance, braking, handling, refinement, and its new interior and exterior appearance. But they also found the seats insufficiently supportive during hard cornering, commented on the car's marked understeer at speed, disliked the long travel of the clutch pedal and were dismayed by the low-geared steering.

In many ways, that first road test was definitive. Subsequent English-language tests added little to it, and even tests of the 3.4-litre and 3.8-litre Automatic models simply seemed to be variations on a theme. The 2.4-litre cars were never given the full road test treatment by a major magazine and after 1963 in any case the focus of new-car interest switched to the S-types. In the public eye, meanwhile, the compact Jaguars continued to be regarded as offering excellent value for money and the 3.8-litre models remained every young man's dream of a fast and stylish saloon car. Yet sales were not always as strong as the cars' legend would suggest.

Mk 2 sales did get off to a good start. Production figures for 1959 show that just over 2,500 cars were built before the end of the year, to keep overall 'compact' totals very similar to the 1958 figures for the older 2.4-litre and 3.4-litre cars. It was 1960

The Mk 2 was very similar to the 2.4-litre and 3.4-litre models which had preceded it, but it was also distinctive in many areas. A comparison of this picture with one of those showing a Mk 1 will make the differences obvious. The overall effect of the styling changes was to make the compact Jaguar appear much lighter and more modern.

Little had changed under the bonnet, however. This is the engine bay of a 3.4-litre Mk 2, pictured in 1960.

before the real impact of the new models was felt, however: production jumped by nearly 55 per cent to meet demand, and some 85 per cent of the increased sales could be accounted for by the new 3.8-litre models. The figures for 1961 were even more impressive, and production was 21 per cent up on 1960 at a total of 21,236.

Yet 1961 was to prove a dramatic peak which Jaguar would never even approach again. For in 1962 sales of the compact models collapsed and only 12,743 cars were built. The reasons are not hard to determine. No sales were yet going to the new Daimler compacts, for only eight had been built during 1962, but in Britain the newly revitalized Rover 3-litre range had begun to take sales away from the Jaguars. Outside Britain, where Rovers counted for very little, new Alfa Romeos (the 2600 saloons and coupés), Fiats (especially the 2300S coupés) and Mercedes-Benz (the 300SE saloons) were probably eating into the Jaguars' market. And in the USA, the first cheap Muscle Cars had put in an appearance, offering enormous straight-line performance even if they handled badly and were crude by Jaguar's standards.

During 1963 Mk 2 production slipped again, although sales lost to Jaguar were largely picked up by the new Daimler 2.5-litre V8 which used the same bodyshell. That year, Daimlers accounted for 19 per cent of total 'compact' production. There were further losses for 1964, balanced out by further defections to Daimler and to the new S-class Jaguars, themselves also derivatives of the Mk 2 compacts. Then 1965 saw another major collapse, orders justifying the production of no more than 4,847 compact Jaguars, some 23 per cent of the total built in the record year of 1961. Daimler production was down that year too, although S-type Jaguar sales hit their peak year and these cars had probably taken many sales away from the Mk 2s.

However, 1966 was a bad year all round. Mk 2 Jaguar production was lower again, Daimler sales slipped and the S-types were now on the downhill slope as well. It was not surprising that Browns Lane took a number of economy measures in the autumn of that year to reduce the production cost of the Mk 2s, as low production meant that each car cost correspondingly more to manufacture. By the time Mk 2 production stopped in mid-1967, in favour of the further cheapened 240 and 340 models, the public was more than ready for the all-new Jaguar which would appear as the XJ6 in 1968.

In terms of individual models, the 3.4-litre cars sold most overall, but they were not always the most popular. In 1959, for example, they were bested by the 2.4-litre cars, in 1962 by the 3.8-litres, and in 1960 and 1961 they were outsold by both 2.4 and 3.8 types. Second most numerous overall were the 3.8-litre cars, which were the best sellers in 1961 and 1962; but their peak years were followed by a sharp decline and they probably lost many sales to the new S-types after 1963.

Least numerous were the 2.4-litre cars, although in fact only about 3,200 cars separated them from the total for the best-selling 3.4-litres. They started out as the best sellers in 1959 and 1960, which was surprising because the 3.4-litre models had been the stronger sellers of the two old models: perhaps the increased cost of the Mk 2 cars was a factor here. In 1961 they took second place to the 3.8-litre models, and then in 1962 began a gradual decline, besting the 3.8-litres only in 1966 and 1967 and never again outselling the 3.4-litre cars.

PRODUCTION CHANGES, 1959–1967

In the eight years of their production, scores

The Mk 2 could be had with a 3.8-litre engine as well as the 2.4-litre and 3.4-litre types. Distinguishing features were few, but included this proud grille badge.

A 3.8-litre Mk 2 pictured in 1994.

Mk 2 production figures

Calendar year	2.4-litre	3.4-litre	3.8-litre	Total
1959	1,119	748	665	2,532
1960	6,717	5,284	5,534	17,535
1961	6,459	6,050	8,727	21,236
1962	3,358	4,660	4,725	12,743
1963	2,857	4,155	3,241	10,253
1964	1,904	3,539	2,631	8,074
1965	1,355	2,091	1,401	4,847
1966	1,592	1,454	689	3,735
1967	961	1,550	235	2,746
Total	26,322	29,531	27,848	83,701

of minor changes were made to the Mk 2 Jaguars and a complete sequential list of these would be extremely tedious to read. Many of these changes were of little consequence to the average owner in the 1960s, although there is no doubt that many enthusiastic owners in the 1990s do like to establish precise details of the components fitted to their cars when they were new. Before catering for them, however, it is valuable to look at the major changes which were made to the Mk 2 models during their production run and to take account of the more visible alterations, both major and minor.

No more than three major changes were made to the Mk 2s in eight years, which is surely a testimony to the excellence of the original design. The first of these came in September 1960, when power-assisted steering was offered as an option for the first time. It was both welcome and long overdue: the compact Jaguars were notorious for their heavy steering, particularly at parking speeds, and the new system removed most of the effort without destroying feedback or making the steering over-light. It was only ever available on the

3.4-litre and 3.8-litre cars, as the lighter engine in the 2.4-litre models made it unnecessary.

There were no more major changes until the summer of 1965, when both manual and automatic transmissions were changed. The automatics came first, the latest Borg Warner type 35 3-speed box taking over from the same company's DG type in June. The main advantage of the type 35 was that it changed up and down more smoothly than the older box. Manual boxes were changed in September, when the old Moss box with its 'crash' first gear was replaced by the latest Jaguar all-synchromesh box already seen in the Mk X and S-type saloons. Once again, the improvement was very welcome, even if the long-travel gearchange could be counted as a disadvantage.

The third and final major changes came in September 1966, when Jaguar introduced a number of economy measures to keep manufacturing costs down and thus to keep the showroom price of the Mk 2 within reasonable bounds. The twin recessed foglamps were replaced by dummy horn grilles (although the lamps could still be had at extra cost), there was a simplified single-piece chrome moulding on the B-pillar, and rubber door seals replaced the weather strip on the chrome beading around the door tops. Inside, Ambla vinyl upholstery replaced the traditional Jaguar leather (which became an extra-cost option) and the picnic tables were deleted from the front seat backs. The material of the head-lining and sun visors was also changed for the cheaper type already seen in the S-type saloons; shortly afterwards, Velcro strip carpet fasteners replaced the stud type used since 1964. Thus reconfigured, the Mk 2 Jaguars remained available until they were replaced in September 1967 by the 240 and 340 models.

Minor, but very visible, changes were far more numerous. They began in 1960, before the Mk 2s had been on the market a full season, when no fewer than five specification changes were made between March and July. First, the dashboard oil pressure gauge was changed from a 100lb type to a 60lb type, the smaller scale allowing the needle to register in the middle of the gauge when all was well and thus preventing owners from worrying unnecessarily!

Next came a telescopic interior mirror, with a wider range of adjustment than the fixed type. The steering column stalks swopped sides in May, allegedly to suit export markets, so that the indicator stalk ended up on the left and the overdrive switch on the right. In July the black-painted centre dash panel was replaced by

The 120mph speedometer gives away that this is a 2.4-litre Mk 2; 3.4-litre and 3.8-litre models had 140mph speedometers. The Mk 2 dashboard was a masterful piece of styling, even if it left a little to be desired in ergonomic terms. This car has no radio and is therefore fitted with a blanking plate over the radio aperture between the heater controls in the console.

a Rexine-covered type because the paint finish had been too prone to scratch damage from ignition keys. And under the bonnet, a paper air filter housed in a large pancake casing with twin trumpets replaced the oil-bath filter on 3.4 and 3.8 engines, though the oil-bath type remained optional.

Shortly after the beginning of the 1961 season in the autumn of 1960, more small changes were made. In November Mk 2s started coming off the lines with modified front door window frames which had been reinforced at their bottom edges. These reinforcements prevented the door frames flexing and being sucked outwards at speed, thus creating wind noise. The original rigidly mounted sun visors had come in for criticism both because they fouled the rear view mirror and because they could not be swivelled to shield the side windows, so swivelling sun visors of a new shape were introduced. The original ashtray tended to deposit its contents all over the floor and so Jaguar biased the spring loading of the lid towards the closed rather than open position.

November also saw the original accelerator pedal replaced by an organ-type pedal, which had been fitted on a few earlier cars and was intended to appeal to more sporting drivers who were unable to heel-and-toe with the older type. New paint colours – including Jaguar's first metallics – were introduced in February 1961, and the 1961 season changes closed with the introduction of a zone-toughened windscreen across the Mk 2 range in June.

The 1962 season was a quiet one and the only visible change was the standardization of seat belt mounting points in deference to the increasing number of customers who wanted these safety items: three years later, they would become a mandatory fitting on all new cars sold in Britain. Car manufacturers were also turning increasingly to sealed-beam headlamps by this

stage, as they offered greater power and longer life than earlier types with bulbs, and so Jaguar followed suit for the 1963 season, making the change on the production lines in September 1962. The new headlamps were recognizable by their convex lenses, whereas the older lamps had flat lenses. Further changes to the range of paint colours on offer were made in October, in time to affect the 1963 models. Then in March 1963, Jaguar modified the backs of the front seats, cutting them away at the bottom to give rear passengers more foot room.

Customers who examined the 1964 model Mk 2s at the Earls Court Motor Show would have seen just one novelty, in the shape of the slightly different steering wheel already fitted to the Mk X and to the brand-new S-type saloons announced at that show. Its spokes were slightly different in shape to the earlier type, and it allowed the horn to be sounded by pressing the centre boss as well as the horn ring – a rather more natural movement for angry or frustrated drivers! Improved interior lamps were fitted to the centre pillars in March 1964, and in May there was a running change to the carpets, when single-piece items were fitted in the footwells and the fasteners were changed from the 'bow' type to simpler press studs.

The 1965 season opened with no visible changes except the deletion of the 'Automatic' badge from cars with the Borg Warner transmission. Changes to the paint options were held over until December 1964. The gearbox changes already outlined kept Jaguar busy over the summer of 1965, and there were no further visible changes until April 1966, when the optional heated rear window was given its own switch. Previously, it had been operated directly by the ignition switch, a rather unsatisfactory arrangement and one which other manufacturers had avoided. The change brought

Jaguar into line with standard practice elsewhere in the industry.

For 1967 the 'economy' changes took pride of place when the cars were announced at the Earls Court Motor Show in October 1966. Subsequent changes were to the paint options, in March 1967, and to the wheels in July. The standard steel wheels were replaced by the type used on the 420 models and the optional wire wheels now had forged hubs and straight spokes. Very few cars were built with these final modifications, however.

MINOR RUNNING CHANGES

Many of the more minor running changes to the Mk 2s were made as a result of customer complaints or requests; others were forced on Jaguar by their component suppliers; yet others sprung from problems detected in service; and a final category of changes was prompted by the cost saving to be made from parts commonization with other Jaguar models.

Customer feedback was certainly behind most of the suspension modifications made to improve the Mk 2's handling. Stiffer front springs were specified in May 1960, and 5in wheel rims replaced the original 4.5in size in September that year. February 1961 brought more rigid forged wishbones to replace the pressed type and the stiffer anti-roll bar formerly optional was standardized at the same time. Then a further change was made in February 1963, when stiffer Girling dampers were fitted to reduce fade in hard use.

As early as 1960 Jaguar were well aware that customers found the Mk 2's heating arrangements inadequate. However, they never did manage to sort this out properly, simply advising dealers to make sure that all the heater flaps closed properly to exclude cold air. In July 1960 they added a water valve to the system (which was originally permanently in circuit) to counter the opposite problem of unwanted heat seeping through from the heater when the air flaps were in the 'off' position. After that, however, customer complaints about the heating and ventilating arrangements fell on deaf ears.

Jaguar did listen when their customers raised queries about refinement, though. They dealt with complaints of petrol smells in the car as early as July 1960, fitting a breather pipe to the filler neck and a non-vented filler cap. The modified ashtray lid in November that year, the stiffened window frames to prevent wind noise in the same month and the improved window seals in April 1963 were all typical responses. Rubber buffers fitted to the door sills and bonnet edges in June 1961 were presumably a response to complaints of rattles or chafing. Drilled camshafts were introduced in August 1961 to minimize clatter during cold starts and in April 1962 a two-stage air valve was fitted to the brake servo to prevent the sighing noises during braking about which customers had complained.

Jaguar were also concerned to make routine owner maintenance as easy as possible. In February 1961 they fitted a dipstick guide tube because customers had complained of difficulty in re-inserting the dipstick; then in November 1962 they lengthened the dipstick handle to stop owners burning their hands on the exhaust manifold. The dipstick for the automatic transmission fluid was under the transmission tunnel carpet on the first cars and Jaguar moved this to a more accessible position under the bonnet in June 1961. As access to the optional engine block heater was hindered by the exhaust manifold, its fitting boss was moved to the opposite (right-hand) side of the block in November 1960. And automatic fan-belt tensioners removed one routine chore after October 1961.

The revised oil pressure gauge, new sun visors, Rexine dash covering and organ-type accelerator pedal have already been mentioned, and these were also examples of Jaguar responding to customer feedback. Other examples occurred in November 1960, when the steering column was lowered slightly to give a more comfortable driving position, and in November 1965, when an additional notch in the front quarter vents' opening mechanisms allowed them to be fixed open in two different positions. But one annoyance went unchanged until nearly the end: on many cars, the boot lid would spring open on rough roads taken at speed, and it was not until July 1967 that Jaguar finally provided a better catch to cure the problem.

As improved components became available from their suppliers, so Jaguar fitted them. The most obvious example of this was the arrival of the Borg Warner type 35 automatic transmission in 1965, but there were many others. The paper air filters introduced in May 1960 reflected the industry's move away from the older oil-bath type and disposable oil filters in November 1965 again reflected industry trends. Polythene brake fluid reservoirs in September 1960 and windscreen washer reservoirs in April 1965 arrived because manufacturers were moving away from corrodible steel and breakable glass types respectively.

Other developments in componentry lay behind the change of the fuel pump in November 1960 and of the power-steering pump in August 1961. Cast iron brake callipers instead of the malleable iron type, and improved adjusters from June 1961 showed what Dunlop had been working on; an improved handbrake mechanism in April 1966 was again the result of development by the supplier; and then the switch to Girling brakes in July 1967 came about because Girling had bought out Dunlop's braking interests. Different horns and indicator switches in April 1966 were again dictated by suppliers and, lastly, supply difficulties early in 1964 meant that a number of cars had carpets with PVC heel pads instead of the usual Hardura type.

All kinds of problems were reported by dealers to Jaguar's Service Division, and these resulted in a number of service modifications, some of which made the cars easier to work on while others simply prevented recurrences of isolated failures. Into the first category came the modified oil filter assembly to improve access in November 1960, the self-adjusting handbrake mechanism in August 1961 and front suspension modifications in January 1963 which simplified lubrication maintenance. Sealed-for-life universal joints on the propshaft were a further boon after May 1963 and engine lifting brackets a time-saver after August 1964. Relocated brake bleed nipples in June 1964 also aided the service mechanic and a new front timing cover on the engine that August allowed the seal to be changed without first removing the whole cover. No doubt minor modifications to the exhaust tailpipe as late as December 1966 were intended to make replacement easier.

Cases of failure in service must have prompted Jaguar to introduce water deflectors to protect the front hubs in August 1961, a stronger cast iron crankshaft pulley in place of the alloy original in October that year, waterproofed distributors in April 1963, and shields for the brake discs in October 1964. This latter certainly arose from reports that the inner pads wore faster than the outers. A new top hose and clip, together with a change to a 9lb (4kg) radiator pressure cap in May 1963, were Jaguar's response to overheating problems; they addressed this difficulty again in December 1964 when they fitted bigger radiators and larger fan cowls to all the Mk

2s. Other problems were solved with a larger-capacity oil pump (August 1961), a larger universal joint on the propshaft (December 1961), improved exhaust manifold gaskets (February 1962), and longer main bearing cap dowels on the left-hand side (October 1962).

During 1963 came a Panhard rod mounting bracket reinforcement (January), dust excluders around the headlamps (May), re-routed spark plug leads (September), tougher mounting rubbers for the front cross-member (October), and a rectifier for the clock and stronger bracketry for the brake vacuum tank (November). Jaguar tackled an interesting problem in April 1965 when they had to lengthen the battery tray drain tube to prevent water dripping onto a brake pipe and promoting corrosion, and another odd one surfaced that year when there were reports of rear quarter-vent catches working loose and even falling off. That was solved by adding Loctite glue to the screws during production after November. Then December 1966 saw a simplification on the 2.4-litre engine assembly lines when the crankshaft vibration damper and fan belt pulley were replaced by a pulley with integral damper.

The drain on the electrical system was clearly greater than Jaguar had expected, perhaps because more and more cars were now being equipped with radios, but it must have been most pronounced on those cars with the heated rear window, which was permanently live until April 1966. So a high-output dynamo was made optional on 3.4-litre and 3.8-litre models in February 1962 (presumably the less wealthy owners of 2.4-litre cars could not afford radios or heated rear windows!) and was standardized on all three models from April the following year.

Oil loss from the engines remained a problem throughout production of the Mk 2 and the first attempt to deal with it came in January 1960, when sump sealing was improved. Oil tended to seep from the rear of the engines when cars were parked facing uphill, so in January 1961 Jaguar modified the crankshaft rear cover. But the problem did not go away until the scroll type oil seal at the back of the engine was replaced by a rope type in October. In December a new cover was added over the exhaust camshaft to improve oil sealing; the change from a four-bolt oil filter casing to a five-bolt type in November 1962 may well have been yet another attempt to make the engines oil-tight. Meanwhile, the 3.8-litre engines had gained a reputation for burning oil and Jaguar tackled that first by fitting new scraper rings to the pistons in September 1962, and then in January 1964 by modifying the pistons themselves. The modified type had a chamfer and drain holes below the oil control ring, to enable surplus oil to drain back into the sump. Even then, oil consumption remained quite high and the exhaust of a 3.8-litre engine in tip-top condition has always had a bluish tinge.

During the 1950s the compact Jaguars had been the new models in the range, and thus tended to be the first with new features which were later carried over to other models. By the 1960s, however, there were newer models in the range, and the new features were tried out on these first and carried over to the Mk 2s later. Relatively few features filtered down from the Mk X saloon introduced in 1961 and only the optional close-ratio gearbox came from the E-type introduced the same year, but the arrival of the S-type compacts in 1963 had a more marked effect on the Mk 2s.

Parts commonization with the Mk X started in 1963, when the bigger saloon's steering column was fitted to Mk 2s in March and its falling-flow water pump fitted to 3.4-litre and 3.8-litre Mk 2 engines in May. In October the Mk X type steering wheel went into the new S-types and the Mk 2s simultaneously, and thereafter it was the S-type which led the way. Mk 2s picked up S-type fuel pumps in March 1964, S-type oil cleaners and flywheels that April, and then took on the S-type's 4lb (1.8kg) radiator pressure cap and fused overdrive circuit (or intermediate-hold circuit in automatics) in May. In October 1964 it was the S-type sump pan; in September 1965 it was the all-synchromesh gearbox (first seen on the Mk X); and in March 1967 it was the Varamatic power steering. The 420 also had its effect on the Mk 2s, which in July 1967 picked up the newer car's overdrive telltale (with a red light to indicate when the overdrive was engaged) and its new disc wheels.

THE MK 2s ON THE ROAD

Jaguars had always been driver's cars above all else, and the Mk 2 compacts were no exception. The undoubted star of the range was always the 3.8-litre overdrive model, which delivered astonishing acceleration for the time together with a maximum speed beyond the wildest dreams of the average motorist. However, that maximum speed was rarely usable – especially in Britain after the introduction of a 70mph (110km/h) limit in 1965 – and in many respects the 3.4-litre model was therefore a more realistic proposition. In overdrive form it was as fast as an automatic 3.8, and many people have argued that the 3.4-litre engine was always the sweetest of the XK types.

By contrast, the 2.4-litre Mk 2 was not a high-performance car. Even in manual form, it was sluggish, while in automatic form it was frankly slow – which no doubt explains why so few 2.4 Automatics were sold. Yet the 2.4-litre car did sell well, and that was because it shared with its bigger-engined sisters all the other charms of the Mk 2 range.

Optional extras for Mk 2 Jaguars

Ace Turbo wheel trims
Childproof locks for rear doors
Column-mounted combined ignition and starter switch
Competition wire wheels (in body colour or silver stove enamel only)
Foglamps (standard on some models)
Heated rear window
Laminated windscreen
Lockable fuel filler cap
Power-assisted steering
Radio
Radio aerial (for roof or wing; also wing-mounted manually retractable type with winding handle under dash)
Radio speaker for rear shelf, with balance control
Reclining front seats
Reclining front seat kit (to convert fixed type to recliners)
Rimbellishers for wheels
Safety belts (front seats only)
Steel sunroof
Sundym tinted glass
Tow-bar
Wing mirrors (standard or Paddy Hopkirk sports style)
Wire wheels (in body colour, chrome or silver stove enamel)

The wood and leather interior always imparted a feeling of well-being to driver and passengers alike and the large (by the standards of the day) glass area gave the driver a feeling of being in control. That feeling was enhanced by the impressive array of switches and dials on the dashboard. The comfortable seats were a boon,

Jaguar Mk 2 models – typical performance figures

	2.4-litre overdrive	3.4-litre overdrive	3.4-litre automatic
0–60mph	17.5 secs	10 secs	12 secs
0–90mph	45 secs	23.5 secs	26 secs
Top speed	96mph (154km/h)	118mph (190km/h)	113mph (182km/h)
Fuel consumption	18–21mpg (13–16l/100km)	17–21mpg (13–17l/100km)	16–20mpg (14–18l/100km)
	3.8-litre overdrive	3.8-litre automatic	
0–60mph	8.5 secs	10 secs	
0–90mph	18.5 secs	21.5 secs	
Top speed	125mph (201km/h)	120mph (193km/h)	
Fuel consumption	16–19mpg 15–18l/100km)	15–18mpg (16–19l/100km)	

too, although those in Mk 2s never gave as much lateral support during cornering as those in the original compact Jaguars. The switchgear always had a satisfying solidity about it, even though the positions of individual switches definitely had to be learned, and the controls were mostly nicely weighted. However, the steering was still unacceptably heavy at parking speeds unless power-assisted, and the original Moss gearbox in manual cars was no delight to use; the later all-synchromesh Jaguar box was infinitely more pleasant.

Out on the road, the cars could be hustled through corners at a cracking pace, their wider rear tracks giving greater stability than any standard Mk 1 compact ever had. Steering was pleasantly accurate – although not up to the best of the rack-and-pinion systems then coming into vogue – and the optional power assistance did not destroy the feedback from the front wheels which is so essential in a fast car. Stopping was also powerful and reliable, despite the cars' considerable weight.

Nevertheless, drivers were always conscious of that weight. The Mk 2 Jaguars felt nicely solid; they even felt responsive and agile in 3.4-litre and 3.8-litre forms; but they never allowed their drivers to forget how much metal they were moving around. Just as that weight began to count against them in sporting events, so it was one of the factors which eventually made them begin to feel old-fashioned on the road.

RIVALS

Just as the original compact Jaguars had been largely without rivals, so the Mk 2s had almost no serious competition – at least on the home market. Although the £1,100–£1,300 (plus Purchase Tax) bracket in which these cars and their Daimler equivalents competed between 1959 and 1967 was rather more densely populated than it had been in the 1950s, the Browns Lane products continued to stand out because of their unique blend of qualities.

In Britain, the Mk 2 Jaguars and compact Daimlers remained very much more expensive than ordinary family saloons, but still considerably cheaper than the large luxury cars of their day. Their main competition on price came from the big Humber Super Snipe and Rover 3-litre models, although both of these were sedate luxury saloons without the performance pretensions of the Jaguars, and the Rover moved up a rung on the price ladder when the new Mk II models arrived in 1962. Slightly cheaper than the Jaguars was the Vanden Plas Princess 3-litre from BMC, another sedate luxury saloon which presented no real alternative to the Jaguars, while the top-model Ford Zodiac Executive and Wolseley 6/110 briefly moved into the Jaguar price bracket but were once again aimed at a different clientele. Citroën's futuristic DS saloons also came into contention, but their four-cylinder engines and highly individual characters prevented them from being big sellers in Britain.

Italian imports presented a more sporting challenge, but lacked the luxury features of the Jaguars. The Lancia Appia Series III, imported briefly in the early 1960s, never really caught on. Nor did the Fiat 2300, which at least had a six-cylinder engine of comparable size to the smallest Jaguar. Alfa Romeo could offer only the 1,600cc Giulia models at this price level, and despite the cars' excellent performance they had a limited appeal. German offerings were the stolid Mercedes-Benz 190, the small BMW 1500 and, later, the more promising BMW 1800 and 1800TI. However, such cars were always critical rather than sales successes in a Britain still convinced it made the best cars in the world. Sports coupés from Volkswagen and Volvo, in the shape of the Karmann Ghia 1500 and the 1800S respectively, did fall into the same price bracket as the Jaguars but were generally viewed as seriously over-priced and were certainly unable to compete on performance.

Overseas, the story was quite different of course. Import duties, which worked in Jaguar's favour on the home market, worked against them abroad. On price, Jaguar were unable to compete with Mercedes-Benz or BMW in Germany, with Alfa Romeo in Italy or with any number of domestic makers in the USA, where high performance took on a new importance in the 1960s. However, only Jaguar offered the luxury of a wood and leather interior combined with high performance and with seats for five people – the 'Grace, Pace, Space' equation of their advertising – and this uniqueness undoubtedly kept them afloat in highly competitive overseas markets.

THE MK 2 IN THE USA

When the Mk 2 Jaguar was launched in the USA at the end of October 1959, the sales of imported cars in that country were still on the increase and Britain was still the most successful importer. However, things were about to change: the US domestic manufacturers began to fight back strongly during 1959 with the announcement of their new compact sedans – Chevrolet's Corvair, Ford's Falcon and the Plymouth Valiant from Chrysler. Moreover, the success of Volkswagen and Mercedes-Benz meant that the West Germans become the number one importers of cars to the USA during 1960, and they would retain that position for the rest of the decade.

Against this background, the success of the Mk 2 Jaguar says a lot for the work put in by Jaguar Cars, Inc. Recognizing that what sold the cars was a combination of their Britishness (the wood and leather interiors counted for a lot here) and their sporting nature, they decided to import only the top-model 3.8-litre type. Although a few 3.4-litre cars seem to have reached the USA to meet special orders, the 2.4-litre model never did cross the Atlantic. Thus, US customers saw in the compact Jaguar only a high-performance sports saloon and the model's image was not complicated by public awareness of the rather more sedate 2.4-litre model.

In spite of the fact that the 3.8-litre Mk 2 won Best Imported Car awards for several years running, it never did sell in huge numbers in the USA. Precise figures are not available, but if as many as 50 per cent of the 14,758 left-hand-drive cars built between 1959 and 1967 went to the USA, sales volumes would have averaged out at fewer than a thousand cars a year.

No doubt Jaguar would have liked to be able to sell more Mk 2s in the USA, but the fact was that they would have been hard pressed to do so. With a showroom price of around $5,000 in 1960 (including the desirable extras of power steering, automatic transmission and wire wheels), the Mk 2 was simply beyond the reach of most buyers. Few standard-sized American family cars of the time cost more than half that figure, a Chevrolet Corvette roadster cost well under $4,000, while around $5,100 bought into the lower reaches of the Cadillac range. So cost limited sales, which in turn gave the car an exclusivity; Jaguar Cars, Inc. based their sales strategy on this, and of course the Mk 2 thus made its own contribution to

The US market was very important to Jaguar in the 1960s, and the 3.8-litre Mk 2 had been introduced primarily to suit US preferences even though it was also a big hit in most other markets. The whitewall tyres looked even better on a wire-wheeled car.

This 2.4-litre model registered in November 1956 is typical of the original compact Jaguars. In this 1994 picture, the headlamps are the only non-original items visible; early cars like this originally had lamps with flat lenses, whereas those on this car are the later (Mk 2) convex type – apparently with yellow bulbs to suit French driving requirements.

Martin Payne's 1956 2.4-litre Jaguar is finished in Sherwood Green and wears the optional Ace Turbo wheel trims. This car would have been supplied with full spats when new, but it now wears the cutaways which were made optional as a retrospective fitment.

From the rear, both the larger area of glass in the doors and the bigger rear window of the Mk 2 models can easily be seen. This 3.8-litre car is finished in Mist Grey.

From behind, the narrow rear track of the Mk 1 cars is only too apparent.

This 1961 3.8-litre Mk 2 has covered just 30,000 miles (48,000km) from new and is today one of the very finest and most original examples around. Owner Graham Bull has however fitted it with non-original 195/75 whitewall tyres, which make it sit slightly lower than standard. The foglamps in recesses in the front wings were standard on Mk 2s for most markets.

The rear seat of the Mk 2 looks supremely inviting. Note the forward fixing for the wheel spat, visible only when the rear door is open.

Opulent and equally inviting: the dashboard of Graham Bull's 3.8-litre Mk 2.

There is hardly a line out of place in the styling of the Mk 2 Jaguar, here set off to perfection by chromed wire wheels.

Larger rear lights, twin exhaust outlets and a 'Disc Brakes' warning sign in the centre of the bumper all add their own character to the Mk 2.

This delightful 340 wears the optional silver-enamelled wire wheels, which set off its side view to perfection. Strictly speaking, the spinners should be the 'earless' type introduced in 1966; these are the earlier variety.

One of the most flattering views of the compact Jaguars is obtained from the front three-quarters, as this 340 shows.

The third-generation compact Jaguars gained a more modern, lighter appearance through the use of slimmer bumpers like those of the S-type. By this stage, dummy grilles had once again replaced the fog-lamps in the front wings. This 1968 340 belongs to Carl James.

Despite a new name and new badging on the bootlid, the 340 still wore the same grille badge as its 3.4-litre Mk 2 predecessor.

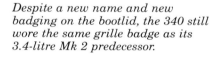

Blue Ambla upholstery complements the Dark Blue paintwork perfectly.

This Daimler V8-250 is finished in Beige (sometimes known as Sable), an attractive colour which suited the shape of the compact saloons very well. The car belongs to Andrew Goddard.

The Daimler's very special character came from its 2.5-litre V8 engine, seen here in V8-250 guise with separate air cleaners for the twin SU carburettors.

The Daimler's interior differed in detail from that of its Jaguar counterparts. Most noticeable in this picture are the 'D' motif on the steering wheel, the perforated leather upholstery, the black Rexine padding on the dash top and the radio panel centre.

The later Daimlers had the same fluted grille as the earlier 2.5-litre V8s, and they retained their fog-lamps when the Jaguars lost theirs. Like the Jaguars, they were given slimline bumpers in 1967. The additional yellow fan visible through the bars of the grille is a non-standard addition.

Distinguishing features of the Daimlers from behind were the V8-250 badge, the fluted lamp housing over the number plate and the dual exhausts, one under each side of the valance panel.

Despite the considerable amount of modifications which have been made to this racing saloon, it is still readily recognizable as a compact Jaguar.

Under the bonnet – which lifts off in true racing style – is where the most important modifications have been made. However, the only non-standard items visible without a close inspection are the big 2in (50mm) SU carburettors.

the wider image of the Jaguar marque in the USA.

Few things illustrate the US sales strategy better than the special car which was built for the 1960 New York Motor Show. This was the brainchild of US Advertising Manager Everett Martin, who wanted a striking centrepiece for the Jaguar stand at this important event. What he actually did was to take a white 3.8-litre Mk 2 and to have every piece of external chrome plate on it replaced by gold plate. For press photographers at the show's opening, the car was accompanied by an elegant model wearing a complementary formal gown of 24-carat gold thread and a Napoleonic tiara containing over 1,000 diamonds. The image created was unforgettable: here was a car intended for the wealthy few. (The car, incidentally, was stripped of its gold fittings before sale, and has now disappeared.)

The actual announcement of the Mk 2 3.8-litre Jaguar in the USA had nevertheless been made some months earlier, on Thursday, 29 October 1959 at Jaguar Cars, Inc.'s New York showrooms on East 57th Street and Madison Avenue. This was just a week after the Mk 2 had been introduced at the Earls Court Motor Show in London and it was in fact the first public showing anywhere for the 3.8-litre model, which had not been on the Earls Court stand. Also exclusive to the US market at this stage was the option of power-assisted steering, which would not be made available elsewhere until February 1960. So it is quite clear that Jaguar recognized the need to treat the American market as a special case even at this early date.

However, there were only two special features on the US-model 3.8-litre car which distinguished it from other left-hand-drive models. These were plain glass lenses (instead of amber) in the front indicator lamps and dummy air-intake grilles in the front wing recesses which normally housed additional driving lamps. After September 1965 all Mk 2s destined for the USA also had a hazard warning light system, which was not available in other countries. Otherwise, American-market cars just drew upon the range of options available elsewhere. Most examples had automatic transmission, power-assisted steering and wire wheels, and probably the majority of cars were also delivered with the whitewall tyres so popular in the USA during the 1960s. Many cars were also fitted with after-market air conditioning installations, but these often had the disadvantage of taking up an unacceptable amount of space in the luggage boot.

By the time the 3.8-litre Mk 2 went out of production in 1967, the US Government had already announced the first of its new measures obliging motor manufacturers to tighten up on safety features and exhaust emissions. The Mk 2 disappeared before these new regulations came into force and so it was never developed to meet them. Whether it could have met them without major modifications is a question Jaguar enthusiasts will probably debate hotly for as long as there is interest in the Mk 2.

THE SOUTH AFRICAN MK 2s

Although some early Mk 2 Jaguars were exported to South Africa, local trade regulations later made it advantageous for car makers to operate assembly plants in that country. Jaguar's plant was established by CDA, at East London, and during the 1960s turned out examples of 2.4, 3.4 and 3.8-litre Mk 2s for local consumption.

The cars were shipped out from Browns Lane in CKD form. Before long, assembly of the 2.4-litre models was stopped, but the 3.4 and 3.8 models remained until the end. A grand total of 2,050 Mk 2 Jaguars was built in South Africa.

Mk 2 Jaguar assembly in South Africa. The cars were built alongside Fiats and Renaults at the East London plant.

THE COOMBS MK 2s

Jaguar dealers Coombs and Son (Guildford) Ltd had started modifying cars for racing in 1958 and had built three competition machines out of early 3.4-litre models. By 1960 they were prepared to offer their expertise to modify customers' cars, and over the next seven years they modified between thirty and forty Mk 2s.

Most of the Coombs Jaguars were 3.8-litre models, although a handful of 3.4s were also converted. Essentially, the Coombs conversion consisted of an uprated engine matched by steering and suspension modifications, but the company offered a variety of options and there was no such thing as a 'standard' Coombs specification.

On top of the basic modifications, Coombs customers could also order items such as an additional fuel tank, a wood-rim steering wheel and a chrome-plated boot rack. Coombs would also modify the rear wheel arches, deleting the spats and making up rolled edges to match the profile of the front wheel arches. This improved the appearance of the car so much that it is surprising Jaguar themselves did not follow suit.

Not all Coombs cars had the same state of tune, but their full-house 3.8-litre car was fast enough to keep pace with a 3.8-litre E-type up to 100mph (160km/h). Not surprisingly, the Coombs cars are very much sought after today, and the absence of any complete set of build records has also led to the creation of some fakes.

One of the distinctive features of a Coombs-modified Mk 2 was the shape of the rear wheelarch. This 3.8-litre model shows just how good the car looked with the Coombs modification – better than the factory original, in fact.

THE MK 2 ESTATE

Jaguar never did produce an alternative body style for the Mk 2, but in 1962 they did buy a prototype estate conversion which was the brainchild of motor racing artist Roy Nockolds and the racing driver Duncan Hamilton. Jaguar used the car, which was known as the Jaguar County, as a support tender for various competition events in Europe in the early 1960s. However, there never seems to have been any plan to put it into production. By the time it was built, Browns Lane was already preparing the introduction of the S-type, and shortly after that, work began on the car which would become the XJ6; as a result, there was never enough engineering time or production capacity to build such a variant in quantity.

The County's origins can be traced back to the late 1950s, when Duncan Hamilton and Mike Hawthorn agreed that a Jaguar estate would be a useful vehicle. Hamilton had already had two Mk VII Jaguars converted to estate cars, and he approached Sir William Lyons with the idea that Jaguar should include an estate car in their range. Lyons was not convinced that there would be sufficient demand, but Hamilton and Hawthorn decided to go ahead on their own and called in Roy Nockolds to advise on styling. Their plan at the time was to base an estate on the original 3.4-litre Jaguar.

After Hawthorn was killed early in 1959, the project lost its impetus for a time.

However, it was revived a couple of years later and during 1962 Jones Brothers (Coachbuilders) Ltd were charged with building a prototype. The car left Jaguar as a 3.8-litre overdrive model in January 1962 (chassis number 207515 DN), finished in British Racing Green and upholstered in Tan. An entry in the Jaguar despatch records suggests that Coombs of Guildford had a hand in its movements over the next few months, but it was not registered (as 3672 VC) until it returned to Jaguar as a works car in September.

The County estate finished its days at Browns Lane as a factory hack and was then sold on to racing driver John Pearson. During the 1970s it was sold to a Jaguar enthusiast, who restored it and converted it from steel to wire wheels. Towards the end of the decade, it changed hands yet again and went to the USA.

POLICE MK 2s

As more and more miles of motorway opened up in Britain during the 1960s, so the need arose for very different types of police patrol car from those which had been common in the 1950s. As motorway patrol cars needed to carry special equipment and to be capable of higher speeds than their urban equivalents, it became general practice for forces with motorway responsibilities to operate fleets of dedicated motorway cars. As the traditional black of the police patrol car was considered too inconspicu-ous, these motorway patrol cars were finished in white.

The Jaguar Mk 2, particularly in 3.8-litre form, proved ideal as a motorway patrol car. It was fast enough for high-speed chase duties, and its good road-holding and braking gave a valuable safety margin for extreme situations. Cost was of course a deterrent, and so it was not surprising that many police forces changed to cheaper cars as soon as they could (the Triumph 2.5PI and Rover 3500 were the most common replacements for the Mk 2s at the end of the 1960s). Mk 2s were also taken on by some police forces for lower-profile duties and during their heyday in the first half of the 1960s, they were on the strength of no fewer than thirty-seven forces.

The typical motorway patrol 3.8 Mk 2 had a large light box on its roof, bearing police signs and a blue flashing light. It would have large police lettering on its sides and rear, and most had twin chromed air horns and a loud hailer mounted on the front bumper. Inside, the rear seat was often removed to provide additional stowage space for the cones and other road-side paraphernalia needed to cope with motorway problems, while there would be a calibrated speedometer and radio-telephone equipment on the dashboard. Contrary to popular belief, however, the police 3.8s were not specially tuned: at most, some of them had stiffer springs (mainly to offset the weight of the equipment they carried) and an uprated dynamo (to power the additional electrical equipment).

Identification: Jaguar Mk 2 2.4-litre, 3.4-litre and 3.8-litre

Identification numbers are stamped on a plate in the engine compartment, attached to the right-hand inner wing. These numbers are repeated elsewhere as follows.

Car (Chassis, VIN) Number
The car number is stamped in the bonnet catch channel, forward of the radiator header tank. A typical car number would be 202389 BW. This breaks down into three elements:

20	model code (sometimes three digits; see below)
2389	serial number (see below)
BW	transmission type (see below)

Sequences are as follows:

	RHD	LHD
2.4	100001–121768	125001–128405
3.4	150001–172095	175001–181571
3.8	200001–215383	210001–224758

Suffixes are:

BW	Borg Warner automatic gearbox
DN	(Laycock) DeNormanville overdrive

Cars fitted with power-assisted steering have a P prefix; for example, P202389BW.

Engine Number
The engine number is stamped on the right-hand side of the cylinder block above the oil filter, and again at the front of the cylinder head casting, beside the front spark plug hole. A typical engine number would be KG5320/8. This breaks down into three elements:

KG	engine type identifier (see below)
5320	serial number (see below)
/8	compression ratio

Type codes are as follows:

2.4	BG, BH, BJ
3.4	KG, KH, KJ
3.8	LA, LB, LC, LE

Suffixes are:

/7	7:1 compression ratio
/8	8:1 compression ratio
/9	9:1 compression ratio

Body Number

On cars built before 1963, the body number is stamped on a small plate attached to the right-hand side of the scuttle, under the bonnet. It has four or five digits.

On cars built after 1963, the body number is stamped on a small plate attached to the right-hand side of the body behind the rear bumper. (It should not be confused with a similar plate on the left-hand side which gives the Pressed Steel reference number.)

Gearbox Number

The gearbox number of manual and overdrive gearboxes is stamped on a small shoulder at the left-hand rear corner of the gearbox and on the rim of the core plug aperture on the top cover. The gearbox number on cars with automatic transmission is stamped on a plate attached to the left-hand side of the transmission casing.

Jaguar 2.4-litre Mk 2 (1959–1967)

Layout

Monocoque bodyshell with front subframe bolted in place. Five-seater saloon, with front engine and rear wheel drive.

Engine

Type	XK, twin overhead camshaft
Block material	Cast iron
Head material	Aluminium alloy
Cylinders	Six, in line
Cooling	Water
Bore and stroke	83 × 76.5mm
Capacity	2,483cc
Main bearings	Seven
Valves	Two per cylinder
Compression ratio	8:1 (7:1 and 9:1 optional)
Carburettors	Two 44mm Solex
Max. power	120bhp @ 5,750rpm
Max. torwue	144lb/ft @ 3,00rpm

Transmisson

Manual models	Hydraulically operated single dry plate clutch, 10in diameter
Automatic models	Torque converter

Internal gearbox ratios
Option 1   Four-speed manual
Top	1.00:1
Third	1.28:1
Second	1.86:1
First	3.37:1
Final drive	4.27:1

(All-synchromesh gearbox with the same internal ratios fitted from September 1965.)

Option 2   Four-speed manual with overdrive
Overdrive	0.77:1
Top	1.00:1
Third	1.28:1
Second	1.86:1
First	3.37:1
Final drive	4.55:1

(All-synchromesh gearbox with the same internal ratios fitted from September 1965.)

Option 3   Three-speed automatic
Top	1.00:1
Intermediate	1.45:1
First	2.39:1
Final drive	4.27:1

Suspension and steering
Front	Independent, with wishbones, coil springs and anti-roll bar
Rear	Live axle with radius arms, Panhard rod and semi-elliptic leaf springs
Steering	Recirculating ball, worm-and-nut; power assistance optional
Tyres	6.40 × 15
Wheels	Five-stud disc type; optional wire-spoke type
Rim width	4.5in to September 1960; 5in after September 1960 and all wire-spoke wheels

Brakes
Type	Servo-assisted discs front and rear
Size	Front 11in, rear 11.375in

Dimensions (in/mm)
Track, front	55.0/1,397 (55.5/1,410 with wire wheels)
Track, rear	53.375/1,355 (53.875/1,368 with wire wheels)
Wheelbase	107.375/2,727
Overall length	180.75/4,591
Overall width	66.75/1,695
Overall height	57.75/1,467
Unladen weight	3,192lb/1,448kg

Jaguar 3.4-litre Mk 2 (1959-1967)

Layout
Monocoque bodyshell with front subframe bolted in place. Five-seater saloon, with front engine and rear wheel drive.

Engine
Type	XK, twin overhead camshaft
Block material	Cast iron
Head material	Aluminium alloy
Cylinders	Six, in line
Cooling	Water
Bore and stroke	83 × 106mm
Capacity	3,442cc
Main bearings	Seven
Valves	Two per cylinder
Compression rario	8:1 (7:1 and 9:1 optional)
Carburettors	Twin SU HD6
Max. power	210bhp @ 5,500rpm (with 8:1 compression)
Max. torque	216lb/ft @ 3,000rpm

Transmission
Manual models	Hydraulically operated single dry plate clutch, 10in diameter
Automatic models	Torque converter

Internal gearbox ratios
Option 1   Four-speed manual
(Figures for close-ratio gearbox in brackets)
Top	1.00:1
Third	1.28:1 (1.21:1)
Second	1.86:1 (1.36:1)
Frist	3.37:1 (2.98:1)
Final drive	3.54:1

Option2   Four-speed manual with overdrive
(Figures for close-ratio gearbox in brackets)
Overdrive	0.77:1
Top	1.00:1
Third	1.28:1 (1.21:1)
Second	1.86:1 (1.36:1)
First	3.37:1 (2.98:1)
Final drive	3.54:1

Option 3   Three-speed automatic
Top	1.00:1

Intermediate	1.21:1
First	1.36:1
Final drive	3.54:1

Suspension and steering

Front	Independent, with wishbones, coil springs and anti-roll bar
Rear	Live axle with radius arms, Panhard rod and semi-elliptic leaf springs
Steering	Recirculating ball, worm-and-nut; power assistance optional
Tyres	6.40 × 15
Wheels	Five-stud disc type; optional wire-spoke type
Rim width	4.5in to September 1960; 5in after September 1960 and all wire-spoke wheels

Brakes

Type	Servo-assisted discs front and rear
Size	Front 11in, rear 11.375in

Dimensions (in/mm)

Track, front	55.0/1,397 (55.5/1,410 with wire wheels)
Track, rear	53.375/1,355 (53.875/1,368 with wire wheels)
Wheelbase	107.375/2,727
Overall length	180.75/4,591
Overall width	66.75/1,695
Overall height	57.75/1,467
Unladen weight	3,304lb/1,499kg

Jaguar 3.8-litre Mk 2 (1959–1967)

Layout

Monocoque bodyshell with front subframe bolted in place. Five-seater saloon, with front engine and rear wheel drive.

Engine

Type	XK, twin overhead camshaft
Block material	Cast iron
Head material	Aluminium alloy
Cylinders	Six, in line
Cooling	Water
Bore and Stroke	87 × 106mm
Capacity	3,781cc
Main bearings	Seven
Valves	Two per cylinder
Compression ratio	8:1 (7:1 and 9:1 optional)
Carburettors	Twin SU HD6

Max. power	220bhp @ 5,500rpm (with 8:1 compression)
Max. torque	240lb/ft @ 3,000rpm

Transmission

Manual models	Hydraulically operated single dry plate clutch, 10in diameter
Automatic models	Torque converter

Internal gearbox ratios

Option 1 Four-speed manual
(Figures for close-ratio gearbox in brackets)

Top	1.00:1
Third	1.28:1 (1.21:1)
Second	1.86:1 (1.36:1)
First	3.37:1 (2.98:1)
Final drive	3.54:1

Option 2 Four-speed manual with overdrive
(Figures for close-ratio gearbox in brackets)

Overdrive	0.77:1
Top	1.00:1
Third	1.28:1 (1.21:1)
Second	1.86:1 (1.36:1)
First	3.37:1 (2.98:1)
Final drive	3.77:1

Option 3 Three-speed automatic

Top	1.00:1
Intermediate	1.45:1
First	2.39:1
Final drive	3.54:1

Suspension and steering

Front	Independent, with wishbones, coil springs and anti-roll bar
Rear	Live axle with radius arms, Panhard rod and semi-elliptic leaf springs
Steering	Recirculating ball, worm-and-nut; power assistance optional
Tyres	6.40 × 15
Wheels	Five-stud disc type; optional wire-spoke type
Rim width	4.5in to September 1960; 5in after September 1960 and all wire-spoke wheels

Brakes

Type	Servo-assisted discs front and rear
Size	Front 11in, rear 11.375in

Dimensions (in/mm)

Track, front   55.01,397 (55.5/1,410 with wire wheels)
Track, rear   53.375/1,355 (53.875/1,368 with wire wheels)
Wheelbase   107.375/2,727
Overall length   180.75/4,591
Overall width   66.75/1,695
Overall height   57.75/1,467
Unladen weight   3,360lb/1,524kg

Colours and trims – Jaguar Mk 2 models

There is some controversy over the colours and trims available during the production run of the Mk 2 Jaguars, not least because Browns Lane was prepared to supply cars painted and trimmed to special order. Catalogues and Service Bulletins issued at various times also often seem to be contradictory! For that reason, this list should be treated with some caution.

October 1959 to January 1961
There were eight standard paint colours, and two extra-cost options were listed. There were six interior trim colour options.

British Racing Green	with trim in	Champagne, Suede Green or Tan
Carmen Red		Black or Red
Cotswold Blue		Dark Blue or Grey
Dove Grey		Grey, Red or Tan
Imperial Maroon		Red
Old English White		Red or Tan
Pearl Grey		Dark Blue, Grey, Light Blue or Red
Sherwood Green		Suede Green or Tan

Special order colours:
Embassy Black	Red or Tan
White	No details

February 1961 to November 1964
There were fourteen standard paint colours, of which six were new metallic finishes (known to Jaguar as 'opalescent' paints). Two extra-cost optional colours were also listed; one (White) was probably mainly specified on police cars. The same six interior trim colours remained available.

British Racing Green	with trim in	Champagne, Suede Green or Tan
Carmen Red		Black or Red
Cotswold Blue		Dark Blue or Grey
Dove Grey		Grey, Red or Tan
Imperial Maroon		Red
Old English White		Red or Tan

Opalescent Blue		Dark Blue, Grey, Light Blue or Red
Opalescent Bronze		Red or Tan
Opalescent Dark Green		Champagne, Suede Green or Tan
Opalescent Gunmetal		Red or Tan
Opalescent Silver Blue		Dark Blue, Grey, Light Blue or Red
Opalescent Silver Grey		Grey, Red or Tan
Pearl Grey		Dark Blue, Grey, Light Blue or Red
Sherwood Green		Suede Green or Tan

Special order colours:

Embassy Black		Red or Tan
White		No details

December 1964 to March 1966

There were ten standard paint colours, of which five were metallic finishes. Two optional colours were also listed; one (White) was probably specified mainly on police cars. There were nine interior trim colours:

Carmen Red	with trim in	Beige or Red
Cream		Dark Blue, Light Blue or Red
Dark Blue		Grey, Light Blue or Red
Opalescent Dark Green		Beige, Light Tan, Suede Green or Tan
Opalescent Golden Sand		Light Tan or Red
Opalescent Maroon		Beige or Maroon
Opalescent Silver Blue		Dark Blue or Grey
Opalescent Silver Grey		Grey, Red or Tan
Sherwood Green		Light Tan, Suede Green or Tan
Warwick Grey		Red or Tan

Special order colours:

Embassy Black		Red or Tan
White		No details

April 1966 to August 1966

Colours and trims remained unchanged except that Black was now listed among the standard colours. There were therefore now eleven standard paints, including five metallics, plus one special option.

Black	with trim in	Grey, Light Tan, Red or Tan
Carmen Red		Beige or Red
Cream		Dark Blue, Light Blue or Red
Dark Blue		Grey, Light Blue or Red
Opalescent Dark Green		Beige, Light Tan, Suede Green or Tan
Opalescent Golden Sand		Light Tan or Red

Opalescent Maroon	Beige or Maroon
Opalescent Silver Blue	Dark Blue or Grey
Opalescent Silver Grey	Grey, Red or Tan
Sherwood Green	Light Tan, Suede Green or Tan
Warwick Grey	Red or Tan

Special order colours:
White	No details

September 1966 to February 1967
Colours and trim colours were unchanged, although Ambla upholstery now became standard and leather became an extra-cost option.

March 1967 to August 1967
The colour range was reduced to just eight standard colours. None of these were metallics. Interior trim materials and colours remained as before:

Beige	with trim in	Light Tan, Red, Suede Green or Tan
Black		Grey, Light Tan, Red or Tan
British Racing Green		Beige, Light Tan, Suede Green or Tan
Carmen Red		Beige or Red CreamDark Blue, Light Blue or Red
Dark Blue		Grey, Light Blue or Red
Warwick Grey		Dark Blue, Light Blue or Tan

7 The 240 and 340

By 1967 Browns Lane had recognized that its saloon range was becoming too complicated. That year began with 2.4-litre, 3.4-litre and 3.8-litre Mk 2s, 3.4-litre and 3.8-litre S-types, and 4.2-litre 420s. Then, of course, there were Daimler V8s and Daimler Sovereign versions of the 420, plus the big Mk X-derived 420G! There were so many illogical overlaps within this range that some form of slimming-down was the only sensible way forward.

So for the 1968 season Jaguar rationalized their saloon ranges. With the elimination of the 3.8-litre Mk 2 and some price adjustments, the company removed the overlap between the top end of the old Mk 2 range and the bottom end of the S-type range. And, following the process which had already begun with the final Mk 2s, Browns Lane trimmed the specification of the remaining 2.4-litre and 3.4-litre compacts in order to keep manufacturing costs within bounds and permit the keen pricing on which the company had always depended.

With effect from the end of September 1967, the compact saloons were renamed 240 and 340 respectively, following the new policy established with the 420 and 420G a year earlier. (At Browns Lane, however, they seem to have been known as 'Mk 2 240' and 'Mk 2 340' models.) According to John Dugdale's book, *Jaguar in America,* this policy of using numbers rather than capacity sizes to designate different models was adopted to help Jaguar's American sales. In the USA Mercedes-Benz had (unintentionally) created a certain mystique with their use of model numbers such as 250SE and 300SE and Jaguar wanted to follow suit! However, it was not a policy which would last for long: engine capacities were given in litres once again when the new XJ6 models reached the market in autumn 1968.

The 240 and 340 models were easily distinguished from their Mk 2 predecessors by their slimmer bumpers. Those at the front were borrowed intact from the S-type cars, and although the matching rear bumper was unique to the 240 and 340 (and their Daimler equivalents) it did wear S-type overriders. Both front and rear valance panels were modified to suit. Metallic paints disappeared from the options list, to be replaced by a selection of attractive new solids. In addition, the 240 and 340 Jaguars had new hub-caps with black plastic badges in the centre, exactly like those first seen in 1966 on the 420 and 420G models. Boot-lid badging reading '240' or '340' completed the exterior transformation, other details like the dummy horn grilles being exactly the same as on the final Mk 2s.

Also like the final Mk 2s, the 240 and 340 saloons came with Ambla upholstery as standard, although leather was still available at extra cost. Picnic tables in the backs of the front seats were not available, however, even as an option. Carpets, too, were cheaper than before, now being made of tufted nylon instead of wool; and the wood trim now came in a lighter shade with less prominent figuring – a sign of changing public tastes. Manufacturing costs had been saved even in the boot, where there was a

The new S-type bumpers and overriders successful-ly made the cars look lighter than before and – to some eyes – even more attractive. Those dummy horn grilles were not the same as the grilles seen on Mk 1 cars in the 1950s.

There was discreet new badging on the bootlid, although the new models still had the same grille badges as their predecessors.

Interiors, too, appeared just as luxurious and well-appointed as before. Only a closer look would reveal that the figured wood trim was matched not by leather but by Ambla plastic upholstery.

moulded plastic tool box instead of the wood-and-metal type supplied with earlier compacts.

It was unfortunate that these were the changes which attracted most attention, even if it was understandable because they were visible and obvious. Many people who had not noticed the cheapening process start with the final Mk 2s (when the changes had received little media attention) did notice what was happening when the 240 and 340 were introduced, and some of them complained bitterly and publicly. They should have looked a little more

deeply, because both models had been given very worthwhile mechanical updates.

The more significant changes had been made for the 240, whose engine now boasted a power increase to 133bhp from the 120bhp of the Mk 2 2.4, together with increased torque of 146lb/ft at 3,700rpm (up from 144lb/ft at 3,000rpm). The main benefits of this were that the car could now exceed 100mph (160km/h) with ease for the first time and that its acceleration at high speeds was improved. The extra power and torque had been achieved by fitting the straight-port cylinder head as used in the E-type 4.2-litre engine in place of the old B-type cylinder head.

In addition, the 240 engine had a new water-heated inlet manifold, which bore twin SU HS6 1.75in carburettors instead of the Solexes always used on the 2.4-litre engines. A paper-element air cleaner was mounted transversely on the engine in place of the rather restrictive oil-bath type and, to complete the transformation, a new dual-pipe exhaust system was fitted in place of the earlier single-pipe type.

The 3.4-litre engine had also been modified. Like the 240, the 340 had a straight-port cylinder head and a paper-element air cleaner (in this case taken from the S-type and slightly different from the 240's). Although Jaguar did not claim any power or torque increases over the Mk 2, comparisons suggested that the new 340 was noticeably quicker than the old 3.4-litre car. Both 240 and 340 engines sported the latest style of ribbed camshaft covers, both of them had distributors with side-entry rather than top-entry leads, and both of them had a new thermostat arrangement in their cooling systems. This closed off the radiator by-pass when it opened, thus allowing the full flow of coolant from the water pump to pass through the radiator for more effective cooling without an increase in radiator size. Servicing inter-

Looking at this 240, it is hard to realize that it had been the subject of a careful cost-paring exercise. The cheapest model of the Jaguar range still looked elegant.

vals for both engines had been increased from 2,500 to 3,000 miles (4,000 to 5,000km) – an improvement, but still not up with the leaders in 1967.

Like the 2.4-litre Mk 2 which it replaced, the new Jaguar 240 could still be obtained in three basic variants, with manual, manual-plus-overdrive, or automatic transmission. The earlier 2.4-litre Mk 2 had never sold very well in automatic form, but Jaguar announced that supplies of the automatic 240 would be more plentiful – their way of saying that they hoped it would be more popular because its revised engine gave better performance. The 340 came with the same three transmission options,

making a total of six versions of the compact Jaguars. In addition (as related in Chapter 8), there were three versions of the Daimler V8-engined car. So despite an apparently slimmer range, there were still no fewer than nine different compacts available from Browns Lane!

Perhaps most striking of all was the pricing of the new models. The much-improved 240 cost £23 more than the superseded 2.4 Mk 2, but in automatic form it now cost £16 less than an automatic 2.4. The 340, meanwhile, cost the same as the last of the 3.4 Mk 2s with manual transmission and in automatic form was £40 cheaper than its Mk 2 equivalent. As ever, the compact

Jaguars represented remarkable value for money, even when compared to more recent designs.

THE 240 AND 340 ON SALE

Although Jaguar listed only the 240 and 340 models after the end of September 1967, the newcomers did not finally supplant the Mk 2s for several months because examples of the older cars lingered on in the showrooms until early 1968. However, the change-over was not as slow as it had been when the Mk 2s had replaced the Mk 1s back in 1959: after a single pilot-build example of each model had been assembled in June 1967, volume production of the 240s and 340s began in mid-August.

Despite some negative public reaction in the beginning, the 240 and 340 models sold steadily. Both were available for the whole of the 1968 season, but production of the 340 stopped in September that year (when the new XJ6 was launched) and sales naturally tailed off. The 240 remained available until the following summer and the last example was built on 9 April 1969, but the 692 cars built in that first quarter suggest that demand was no lower than in the previous year. Nevertheless, the compacts had to go: they were expensive to produce and their fifteen-year-old design was looking increasingly old-fashioned against more modern machinery from rival manufacturers.

PRODUCTION CHANGES, 1967–9

From the beginning of 240 and 340 production, Jaguar knew that the cars would be in production for only a relatively short time. The cost of major changes during the production run would therefore never have been amortized, and so the 240 and 340 models remained very much the same when they were taken out of production as they had been when production had begun. However, detail changes were made from time to time, and for a variety of reasons.

By the late 1960s many countries had started to tighten up on legislation applying to motor vehicles. The pioneers in this respect had been the West Germans (although the US legislation which was announced in the mid-1960s proved more far-reaching in its effects) and other countries began to follow suit. As no two countries' new regulations ever seemed to be alike, this was a difficult period for motor manufacturers who were obliged to produce a given model with a wide variety of different detail specifications.

Some of the changes made to the production specification of the 240 and 340 Jaguars during 1968 reflected the arrival of this new legislation. New West German legislation demanded sidelamps integral with the headlamps, and so from July that year 240s and 340s for West Germany were given new headlamp units with sidelight

Jaguar 240 and 340: production figures

Calendar year	240	340	Total
1967	911	1,005	1,916
1968	2,827	1,799	4,626
1969	692		692
Total	4,430	2,804	7,234

bulbs incorporated in them. The original sidelamp pods remained on top of the wings, but the lamp units were not wired up. A further change in December 1968 illustrated the sort of problems new legislation was beginning to cause: although Jaguar were able to simplify production a little by fitting a common type of 'European' headlamp to left-hand-drive vehicles, Austrian cars now became the exception because they retained the older type of headlamp.

West Germany had already insisted for safety reasons that the knock-on hubcaps which came with wire wheels should not have protruding spinners, and now a new design of knock-on hubcap was standardized to meet new requirements in Denmark, Japan, Sweden and Switzerland. The new hubcap was another July 1968 arrival and was also fitted to cars for West Germany, but all other territories retained the home market type with protruding spinners until production ended. Relatively few cars were affected, in any case, and relatively few cars were affected by the standardization of a cylinder block heater on all cars for Canada in July 1968: the 340s, in particular, had only another two months of production life left.

Stove-enamelled wire wheels were still available for these final models of the compact Jaguars. These are on a 340.

More minor changes were made in six groups between January 1968 and May 1969. The first 'group' was in fact a single change, when renewable petrol filter elements replaced the gauze type. Then from July 1968 all cars were given a new water temperature gauge with simplifed 'Normal' and 'Danger' zone markings instead of the earlier calibrations. Push-fit terminals replaced the screw-in type on coils at the same time and on the 340 engine there were different struts for the oil suction and delivery pipes. These changes affected the very last of the 340s and the cars which would become '1969-model' 240s.

The next group of changes was made in December 1968, by which time only the 240 was left in production. Engines gained sintered valve seats of an improved pattern (in which their depth was reduced); a new type of Lucas starter solenoid was fitted; and there was also a new non-hydrostatic clutch slave cylinder. This was something of a mixed blessing because it did not compensate automatically for clutch wear and thus added one extra chore to the servicing list. Further engine changes arrived in January 1969, when new conrod bolts and nuts with a higher tensile strength were introduced.

The fifth group of changes was made in March 1969. These consisted of a modified gearbox plug on overdrive cars to reduce the risk of the overdrive being starved of oil under certain conditions. Then the final changes were made in May 1969. Jaguar changed the 240's water pump spindle and modified the petrol pipe between filter and float chamber; on left-hand-drive cars they fitted a different choke cable in response to complaints of sticking with the old type.

Lastly, it looks as if a few 240s and 340s may have been fitted with a black PVC padded roll on the tops of their dashboards, exactly like that offered in the contemporary Daimler V8-250. As there is no clear

record of this in Jaguar literature, it is probable that these 'safety' dashboards may have been fitted to special order (if they were indeed original equipment).

Optional extras for 240 and 340 models

Heated rear window
Leather upholstery
Overdrive
Power-assisted steering (340 only)
Radio
Reclining front seats
Seat belts
Special paint finishes
Spotlamps
Wire wheels (chromed or silver
    stove-enamelled only)

THE 340 IN THE USA

Of this final run of compact Jaguars, only the 340 model was made available in the USA. The car was not really perceived as a new model across the Atlantic, but more as a slightly modified 3.4-litre Mk 2. Without a 3.8-litre model in the range, compact Jaguar sales declined in favour of the S-types and 420s, and relatively few of the 535 left-hand-drive 340s built were sold in the USA.

THE 340 3.8

As far as the general public was concerned, the only two engines available for the compact Jaguars in this final phase of their production were the 2.4-litre and 3.4-litre types. However, it appears that Browns Lane remained receptive to special requests and that nine cars were built with 3.8-litre

Inside the boot of this wire-wheeled 340 can be seen the full tool kit and
the rubber-faced hammer which was provided for use on the wheel centre spinners.

Jaguar 240 and 340: typical performance figures

	240 overdrive	*340 overdrive*	*340 automatic*
0–60mph	12.5 secs	8.8 secs	12 secs
0–90mph	30 secs	22 secs	26 secs
Top speed	106mph	124mph	120mph
	(171km/h)	(200km/h)	(193km/h)
Fuel consumption	18–21mpg	17–21mpg	16–20mpg
	(13–16l/100km)	(13–17l/100km)	(14–18l/100km)

engines between December 1967 and May 1968. That total is quoted by Nigel Thorley in his book, *Jaguar Mk I and Mk II – the Complete Companion,* but cannot be substantiated by factory records. Indeed, as far as factory records are concerned, there is no mention of special-order cars at all!

Of the supposed total of nine cars, just one is known for certain to have survived. This has the classic 3.8 Mk 2 specification of an overdrive transmission and wire wheels, and is distinguished by a 3.8-litre grille badge and by chrome '340 3.8' badging on the boot lid. Its engine appears to be a 220bhp 3.8-litre S-type unit, although the engine is numbered in a special sequence.

POLICE MODELS

By the time the 240 and 340 Jaguars came on the scene, the new XJ6 was only just over a year away and Jaguar had no doubt hinted to some of its police customers that they might find the new model very interesting indeed. As the 3.8-litre model which had been a police favourite was no longer available, several forces probably decided to wait for the new model before placing further orders; others, with a more urgent need for new patrol cars, bought stop-gap models from other manufacturers.

There were nevertheless some British forces which found the 240 and (rarely) the 340 adequate for their needs. Naturally, some cars served as unmarked police vehicles, but the majority of the late-model compacts served in the all-white livery of motorway patrol cars. Like their Mk 2 predecessors, they were equipped with loud-hailers, calibrated speedometers, two-way radio equipment and illuminated police signs on the roof, but their precise specification differed from force to force.

THE 240 AND 340 ON THE ROAD

Even though they had lost a number of items of equipment and had smaller bumpers, the 240 and 340 Jaguars were not noticeably lighter than their predecessors in the Mk 2 Jaguar range. However, their revised engines gave them rather better acceleration than the earlier models had boasted, and the 240 was very much quicker than the 2.4-litre Mk 2. It also had a higher top speed, and could reach 100mph (160km/h) much more comfortably than any earlier 2.4-litre engined Jaguar.

Handling, road-holding and comfort levels were exactly as they had been on the Mk 2 cars, but to the eyes of their contemporaries these cars were becoming dated. Their great weight made them feel ponderous by comparison with newer quick saloons, and more modern designs offered greater areas of glass in the cabin and thus better visibility for driver and passengers. Fuel economy and heavy steering were by this time out of step with the latest standards, but were of course no worse than they had been on earlier Jaguars.

RIVALS

Jaguar's policy of keeping showroom prices for the 240 and 340 models as low as possible was something of a double-edged sword. It undoubtedly ensured that these by now elderly models would still find buyers; it undoubtedly maintained the Jaguar traditions of keen pricing and value for money; but it also pitched the compact saloons into a different and much more competitive market sector.

Throughout the 1950s and early 1960s, the Jaguar compacts had occupied an almost unique position in the market. Even though models from other manufacturers offered

Under the bonnet of the 340, there were differences from the earlier 3.4-litre cars. The air filter had changed, and both the 240 and 340 engines had these ribbed camshaft covers. When the car was new, the battery would have been concealed under a black cover.

many of the Jaguars' qualities – and improved on them in some areas – none had been able to offer quite the same blend of qualities and certainly at nothing like the Jaguars' price. However, the early 1960s had seen the growth of a new market sector, for so-called executive cars, just below the price bracket in which the Jaguars sold. Pioneers in that market had been the Rover 2000 and Triumph 2000 saloons, both introduced in 1963, and by the middle 1960s these models had been joined by a swelling crowd of others. Prices in this sector rose, but the prices of Jaguar's compacts remained static, with the result that the 240 and 340 models found themselves competing in this fiercely contested sector of the market.

A look through new-car prices at the 1967 Earls Court Motor Show makes the change quite clear. Inclusive of Purchase Tax but without extras, the compact Jaguars ranged in price from £1,365 for a manual-transmission 240 to £1,537 for an automatic 340. In that price bracket were also included attractive models by BMW, Citroën, Fiat, Ford, Opel, Reliant, Rover, Vauxhall and Volvo. Perhaps it was still true that none of them offered the same blend of qualities as the Jaguars – but in almost every case they were newer designs and that counted for a lot in the fashion-conscious middle 1960s.

For the buyer who wanted a four-seater sports saloon, the Fiat 2300 at £1,354 might

---

Identification: Jaguar 240 and 340

Identification numbers are stamped on a plate in the engine compartment, attached to the right-hand inner wing. These numbers are repeated elsewhere as follows.

Car (Chassis, VIN) Number
The car number is stamped in the bonnet catch channel, forward of the radiator header tank. A typical car number would be 1J30048BW. This breaks down into three elements:

1J	240 or 340 model
30048	serial number (see below)
BW	transmission type (see below)

Sequences are as follows:

	RHD	LHD
240	1J1001–1J4716	1J30001–1J30730
340	1J50001–1J52265	1J80001–1J80535

(The 3.8-litre special-order models appear to have been numbered within the main 340 sequence.)

Suffixes are:

BW	Borg Warner automatic gearbox
DN	(Laycock) DeNormanville overdrive

Cars fitted with power-assisted steering have a P prefix, eg P1J30048BW.

Engine Number

The engine number is stamped on the right-hand side of the cylinder block above the oil filter and again at the front of the cylinder head casting, beside the front spark plug hole. A typical engine number would be 7J2700/9. This breaks down into three elements:

7J	240 or 340 engine
2700	serial number (see below)
/9	9:1 compression ratio

Sequences are as follows:

240	7J1001 upwards
340	7J50001 upwards

Suffixes are:
/7 7:1 compression ratio
/8 8:1 compression ratio
/9 9:1 compression ratio

Body Number

The body number is stamped on a small plate attached to the right-hand side of the body behind the rear bumper. (It should not be confused with a similar plate on the left-hand side which gives the Pressed Steel reference number.)

Gearbox Number

The gearbox number of manual and overdrive gearboxes is stamped on a small shoulder at the left-hand rear corner of the gearbox and on the rim of the core plug aperture on the top cover. The gearbox number on cars with automatic transmission is stamped on a plate attached to the left-hand side of the transmission housing.

Jaguar 240 (1967–1969)

Layout

Monocoque bodyshell with front subframe bolted in place. Five-seater saloon, with front engine and rear wheel drive.

Engine

Type	XK, twin overhead camshaft
Block material	Cast iron
Head material	Aluminium alloy
Cylinders	Six, in line
Cooling	Water
Bore and stroke	83 × 76.5mm
Capacity	2,483cc

Main bearings	Seven
Valves	Two per cylinder
Compression ratio	8:1 (7:1 optional)
Carburettors	Twin SU HS6
Max. power	133bhp @ 5,500rpm
Max. torque	146lb/ft @ 3,700rpm

Transmission

Manual models	Hydraulically operated single dry plate clutch, 10in diameter
Automatic models	Torque converter

Internal gearbox ratios

Option 1 Four-speed manual

Top	1.00:1
Third	1.28:1
Second	1.86:1
First	3.37:1
Final drive	4.27:1

Option 2 Four-speed manual with overdrive

Overdrive	0.77:1
Top	1.00:1
Third	1.28:1
Second	1.86:1
First	3.37:1
Final drive	4.55:1

Option 3 Three-speed automatic

Top	1.00:1
Intermediate	1.45:1
First	2.39:1
Final drive	4.27:1

Suspension and steering

Front	Independent, with wishbones, coil springs and anti-roll bar
Rear	Live axle with radius arms, Panhard rod and semi-elliptic leaf springs
Steering	Recirculating ball, worm-and-nut; power assistance optional
Tyres	6.40 × 15
Wheels	Five-stud disc type; optional wire-spoke type
Rim width	5in

Brakes

Type	Servo-assisted discs front and rear
Size	Front 11in, rear 11.375in

Dimensions (in/mm)

Track, front	55.0/1,397 (55.5/1,410 with wire wheels)
Track, rear	53.375/1,355 (53.875/1,368 with wire wheels)
Wheelbase	107.375/2,727
Overall length	180.75/4,591
Overall width	66.75/1,695
Overall height	57.75/1,467
Unladen weight	3,192lb/1,448kg

The distinctive tail lamps remained unchanged on the final cars, as this 340 shows.

Colours and trims – Jaguar 240 and 340

September 1967 to April 1969

There were six standard exterior colours, none of which were metallics. Four interior trim colours were available. Upholstery was in Ambla, with leather an extra-cost option.

Beige	with trim in	Beige, Black, Blue orRed
Black		Beige, Black, Blue or Red
British Racing Green		Beige or Black
Cream		Beige, Black, Blue or Red
Dark Blue		Beige, Black, Blue or Red
Warwick Grey		Beige, Black, Blue or Red

Jaguar 340 (1967–1969)

Layout
Monocoque bodyshell with front subframe bolted in place. Five-seater saloon, with front engine and rear wheel drive.

Engine
Type	XK, twin overhead camshaft
Block material	Cast iron
Head material	Aluminium alloy
Cylinders	Six, in line
Cooling	Water
Bore and stroke	83×106mm
Capacity	3,442cc
Main bearings	Seven
Valves	Two per cylinder
Compression ratio	8:1 (7:1 optional)
Carburettors	Twin SU HD6
Max. power	210bhp @ 5,500rpm (with 8:1 compression)
Max. torque	216lb/ft @ 3,000rpm

Transmission
Manual	Hydraulically operated single dry plate clutch, 10in diameter
Automatic models	Torque converter

Internal gearbox ratios
Option 1   Four-speed manual
(Figures for close-ratio gearbox in brackets)
Third	1.28:1 (1.21:1)
Second	1.86:1 (1.36:1)
First	3.37:1 (2.98:1)
Final drive	3.54:1

Option 2   Four-speed manual with overdrive
Overdrive	0.77:1
Top	1.00:1
Third	1.28:1 (1.21:1)
Second	1.86:1 (1.36:1)
First	3.37:1 (2.98:1)
Final drive	3.54:1

Option 3   Three-speed automatic
Top	1.00:1
Intermediate	1.21:1
First	1.36:1
Final drive	3.54:1

Suspension and steering

Front	Independent, with wishbone, coil springs and anti-roll bar
Rear	Live axle with arms, Panhard rod and semi-elliptic leaf springs
Steering	Recirculating ball, worm-and-nut; power assistance optional
Tyres	6.40 × 15
Wheels	Five-stud disc type; optional wire-spoke type
Rim width	5in

Brakes

Type	Servo-assisted disc front and rear
Size	Front 11in, rear 11.375in

Dimensions (in/mm)

Track, front	55.0/1,397 (55.5/1,410 with wire wheels)
Track, rear	53.375/1,355 (53.875/1,368 with wire wheels)
Wheelbase	107.375/2,727
Overall length	180.75/4,591
Overall width	66.75/1,695
Overall height	57.75/1,467
Unladen weight	3,360lb/1,524kg

(Note: The special-order 340 3.8 model was identical to the standard 340 except for engine and transmission details, which parallelled those of the Mk 2 3.8-litre car).

still have figured on a short list of possible purchases, but it attracted very few buyers in Britain. The BMW 1800 would certainly have looked attractive at £1,498, for although its spartan interior was no match for the Jaguars', it boasted excellent handling, road-holding and acceleration. Other possibilities would have included the rapid Opel Commodore at £1,380 and the Vauxhall Viscount automatic at £1,483, a large car with acres of interior space and better performance than its barge-like appearance suggested, but without the roadability or refinement of the Jaguars.

New on the scene was the twin-carburettor Volvo 144S at £1,415, no great beauty but very solidly built and inheriting from earlier Volvos good performance, good roadability and excellent build quality. The Rover 2000TC at £1,451 was neatly pitched between the 240 and 340 Jaguars, and allied new levels of performance to the established 2000 qualities of roadability and restrained luxury, although it fell down on refinement; nevertheless, the singlecarburettor 2000 was a very attractive alternative to a 240 at just £1,357. And there was also the Reliant Scimitar coupé with a Ford 3-litre V6 under its bonnet at just £1,516, its main disadvantage being that it had only two doors. By the time of the 1968 Earls Court Show, there was another serious rival for the Jaguars, as well: the Triumph 2.5PI with its fuel-injected six, priced at a few shillings less than £1,450.

Overseas, where Jaguar prices tended to be higher and those of their locally built rivals lower, the 240 and 340 fought a losing

The slimmer bumpers of the final compact Jaguars gave the cars a more modern and rather lighter appearance.

battle. Sales of the 340 held up quite well, but the 240 was outclassed in many markets and was simply not offered in others.

THE END OF PRODUCTION

Jaguar reasoned that there would be no market for their 3.4-litre compact once the new 2.8-litre XJ6 models went on sale towards the end of 1968, and so they halted production of the 340 models at the end of September after some twelve months. The 2.4-litre car, however, was retained as an entry-level Jaguar for a further season, the

last car being built on 9 April 1969 in the anticipation that dealers would have cleared their showrooms of stocks by the autumn and that the focus would then be on the XJ6 models.

Jaguar no doubt decided against having a spectacular Last-of-Line ceremony for the very good reason that the compact Daimlers remained in production (and would do so until the beginning of August). The last of the compact Jaguars therefore came off the line unnoticed by all except a few Jaguar employees. The car itself was sold on through a dealer in the normal way and has now, in all probability, been scrapped.

8 The Daimler Compacts

Daimler did not do well during the 1950s. Recognizing that the market had changed, and that it would no longer be able to survive on sales of the low-volume, high-quality luxury models which had made its reputation in the first half of the century, the company attempted to break into a new market by offering smaller luxury saloons. But cars like the 1953 Conquest did not sell in large enough numbers to keep Daimler's accounts healthy; by 1955 the company was forced to drop its 'middle-class' Lanchester models, and by the middle of 1956 it was clear that the time had come for drastic action. The decision was taken to develop a new saloon with a V8 engine – a configuration almost certainly chosen with thoughts of expansion into the American market in mind.

The Managing Director of the BSA Automotive Division which had owned Daimler since 1910 was then Edward Turner, who had been a noted designer of motorcycle engines earlier in his career. The task of drawing up the new V8 fell to him, and the urgency of the whole operation was probably what persuaded him to take some short cuts. As Brian Long relates in his book, *Daimler V8 SP250*, Turner then owned a Cadillac, and it was Cadillac's well-proven V8 design that he used as a starting point. From this came the decision to set the cylinder banks at 90 degrees to one another and the decision to go for the simplicity of an overhead-valve layout with a single central camshaft operating the valves by pushrods.

Turner's second short cut was to draw on his own earlier work with motorcycle engines. His most highly acclaimed design had been the V-twin engine he had designed for the 1937 Triumph Speed Twin and from this he borrowed the combustion chamber design and certain dimensions which married up happily with the 2.5-litre capacity he wanted for the new Daimler V8 engine. As a result, the new engine came together remarkably quickly. The first drawings for it were done in October 1956, and the first prototype engine was up and running just eight months later. So accomplished was the design, despite its doubtful-sounding origins, that it seems to have needed very little further development.

The first Daimler V8 engine went on mileage test in a Conquest Century saloon during 1957, but Daimler had no intention of updating its existing saloon in this way. What the company wanted was a completely new saloon, and this was given the code-name DN250 when work started on it towards the end of 1958. However, the DN250 – the infamous project based on a Vauxhall Cresta PA bodyshell – did not prosper. By the middle of 1959 (if not earlier) the project was dead.

Meanwhile, Daimler had decided during 1957 that the new V8 engine should also appear in a sports car aimed primarily at the American market and what Daimler called the SP250 was running in prototype form by the beginning of 1958. When the DN250 project was abandoned, the company decided instead to use the SP250

The V8 engine was a tight fit under the bonnet of the Daimler sports car. Note the small air cleaners, which created more induction roar than Jaguar would have wanted for the saloon engine.

chassis and running gear as the basis of a small sports saloon which was given the codename DP250. The prototype Daimler V8 2.5-litre Close-Coupled Saloon was shown on the stand of Hooper, the coach-builders who had made its body, at the 1959 Earls Court Motor Show – the very same show at which the Mk 2 compact Jaguars were announced.

ENTER JAGUAR

However, the DP250 did not progress beyond the prototype stage. Sales of the SP250 sports car, which had been announced at the New York Show in April 1959, failed to live up to expectations and BSA, already disillusioned with Daimler's progress, decided to dispose of its lame duck. Jaguar stepped in and, from the middle of June 1960, all decisions about future Daimler models fell to Sir William Lyons. He hated the productionized DP250 proto-

type he was shown and ordered the whole project to be scrapped; but he did listen when his engineers told him that their tests of the small-block Daimler V8 engine had shown it to be a thoroughly sound and well-engineered product. It may have been at this point that the idea was born of fitting the Daimler V8 into the bodyshell of a compact Jaguar to provide Daimler with the new saloon it had been struggling to create since 1956.

Browns Lane did not take long to get to grips with the idea. The project was allocated the code number ZX530/112 – it never did get a Daimler code, even though Jaguar did call the later Daimler limousine a DS420 – and by November 1960 Phil Weaver's team in the Experimental Department had transplanted a Daimler V8 into one of their existing Mk 1 Jaguar hacks. This car was put through the usual rigorous test procedures over the next sixteen months, and turned in a performance which was very much better than anyone

The 2.5-litre Daimler V8 engine was first seen in the SP250 sports car. This is a 1962 B-specification model.

A very early 2.5-litre V8 model poses for a publicity photograph in 1962. The fluted Daimler grille was by far the most obvious difference from the Jaguar models.

expected. One result seems to have been that Jaguar considered trying out Daimler's bigger V8 in the compact saloons as well. This was a 4.5-litre engine, broadly similar in design to the 2.5-litre type and available in the Majestic Major saloons and limousines which had been announced in 1959. However, the project seems not to have gone beyond the drawing-board: the engine's width would have demanded engine bay changes in the compact bodyshell and there was little point in offering a 220bhp 4.5-litre V8 when the 3.8-litre XK six-cylinder already gave 265bhp. In addition, Jaguar probably had concerns about the cost of putting the 4.5-litre V8 into large-scale production.

The 2.5-litre V8 project did become seri-

ous, however, and the Experimental Department built a second prototype, this time using one of the current production Mk 2 saloons. By this time, the project seems to have attracted the code XDM2. This second prototype was fitted with Borg Warner's latest automatic transmission, the type 35, and the car proved very successful. Its major drawback was a throbbing and intermittent drumming, which Jaguar discovered was caused by flexing of the engine/transmission unit. The problem was quickly solved by fitting a stiffener plate between the bottom of the bellhousing and the sump.

Browns Lane made a few more alterations to make the V8 more suitable for its new task. The cylinder head studs of the

A sectioned display example of the V8 engine with its rocker covers removed to display the valve gear.

The V8 engine's rocker covers were held on by distinctive knurled nuts around the sparking-plug tubes.

Daimler design were replaced by set bolts so that the heads could be removed with the engine still in the car. The water pump was repositioned centrally on the front face of the cylinder block, with split outlets to each bank of cylinders, and an extra pulley was inserted between crankshaft nose and fan to drive the auxiliaries Browns Lane wanted. New exhaust manifolds were also made up, although it must be said that the design of these suggested Jaguar had not been aiming to extract maximum power from the engine: perhaps better-designed manifolds would have given the V8-engined car too much of a performance advantage over the 2.4-litre Jaguar. Browns Lane also wanted to make the engines as smooth as possible by balancing the crankshafts, but the Daimler design allowed insufficient room to do this properly. They therefore slimmed

down the main bearings to make room – a change which caused some problems for Daimler owners as their cars got older.

Meanwhile, Jaguar's stylists made the Mk 2 look like a Daimler by adding a radiator grille with a fluted top, a number plate lamp on the boot lid with similar fluting, a 'flying D' mascot on the bonnet, and 'D' emblems on the wheeltrim centres and on the centre of the rear bumper, in place of the Jaguar models' disc brake warning sign. The wheels had Rimbellishers as standard, whereas these were only ever optional on Jaguars. The boot lid also bore a chromed 'Daimler' script and a stylized 'V8' badge. More practical than cosmetic, the rear valance panel was changed to accommodate the twin exhausts.

The interior remained recognizably Mk 2 Jaguar, but it did have its own special

On the bonnet, a winged D emblem replaced the leaping cat of the Jaguars.

features. Most obvious was the split bench seat at the front, which allowed a third passenger to be carried in the middle if the two seats were adjusted appropriately. There was no centre console between the seats as in the Jaguars, and its absence gave a rather less sporting appearance to the Daimler's passenger cabin. The absence of console of course left nowhere to conceal the rear heating ducts, and so these were simply omitted, leaving the rear seat passengers a little extra legroom as a result. There were no picnic tables on the front seat backs, either: presumably the comfortably-off retired couples at whom the car was aimed were expected to prefer a proper meal at a tea-room!

The dashboard was broadly similar to the Jaguars', with the 120mph speedometer of the 2.4-litre models. However, the rev counter was red-zoned between 6,000 and 6,500rpm instead of between 5,500 and 6,000rpm as in the Jaguars (the V8 was a more free-revving engine than the XK sixes). In the centre, a veneered extension below the main dashboard housed the radio, heater controls and ashtray. The steering wheel was unchanged from the Mk 2 design, except that its centre boss had a gold-on-black 'D' symbol. The only other interior changes were to the headlining, which was sprung into place on the Daimlers; and to the courtesy lights, of which the Daimlers had just three to the Jaguars' four. All Daimlers also appear to have had a heated rear window, which was always an extra-cost option on the Jaguars.

THE 2.5-LITRE V8 ON SALE

The Jaguar Directors were formally told of

the impending new model during February 1962 and the new car entered production only just in time to be on the Daimler stand at the Earls Court Motor Show which opened on 17 October that year. Production was very slow to get under way and only eight cars were built before the end of the year. Most of these actually had modified SP250 engines which were numbered in the five-digit sequence reserved for the sports car, and the proper saloon version of the engine did not become available until December. As far as buyers were concerned, the cars were therefore not available until the beginning of 1963. Road-test examples were not available until even later and it was May 1963 before *Autocar* published the first test of the new Daimler.

The compact Daimler was priced between the 2.4-litre Mk 2 Jaguar and the 3.4-litre, but its market position would not always stay the same. In later years, its price relative to the Jaguars increased – without any visible benefits, either – and by 1964 it had become more expensive than a 3.8-litre Mk 2. All the Daimlers built before 1967 had automatic transmission and a manual alternative was simply not offered. Jaguar's reasoning was that Daimler had been wedded to the idea of automatic (and before

that, semi-automatic) transmissions since the 1930s and that there would simply be no market for a manual car among traditional Daimler customers.

Throughout its production life, the compact Daimler proved an upmarket alternative to cars like the Vanden Plas 1100, Triumph 1300 and Wolseley 1500 for retired couples who wanted something smart, comfortable and quiet. However, the Daimler also offered a fair turn of speed, being faster than the contemporary 2.4-litre Jaguar, and it thus had a special appeal of its own. On price, it competed in the same market as the Jaguars; but there was almost nothing else at that level of the market which appealed to the same type of customer. The car's appeal outside Great Britain was limited and it was never sold in the USA (where the Daimler name had no standing). In consequence, relatively few left-hand-drive examples were made.

Like sales of the Mk 2 Jaguars, sales of the compact Daimlers peaked in the early 1960s and declined quite rapidly after that. Their best year was 1964, when 3,969 were built, but by 1967 (when the total was shared between the original 2.5-litre V8 and the revised V8-250 models), fewer than half that many left the lines at Browns Lane.

Compact Daimler production figures

Calendar year	2.5-litre V8	V8-250	Total
1962	8		8
1963	2,444		2,444
1964	3,969		3,969
1965	3,430		3,430
1966	2,200		2,200
1967	967	803	1,770
1968		2,871	2,871
1969		1,223	1,223
Total	13,018	4,897	17,915

PRODUCTION CHANGES, 1962–1967

Like their Jaguar counterparts, the compact Daimlers underwent very few major changes before 1967, although scores of minor changes were made. The most important changes were made in December 1963, when the latest version of the Borg Warner transmission with its D1/D2 control was fitted, and in February 1967 when a manual gearbox option was introduced for export markets; it was not available on the home market until the following February, by which time the 2.5-litre V8 had become a V8-250. The gearbox fitted came straight out of the 2.4-litre Jaguar and was offered with overdrive at extra cost – although very

few cars had overdrive from new. When overdrive was fitted, a 4.55 axle replaced the standard 4.27 type. The Daimlers never suffered the 'economy' measures introduced on Mk 2 Jaguars in the autumn of 1966, and retained their leather upholstery and fog lamps to the end. Production of the 2.5-litre Daimlers stopped in November 1967, assembly of left-hand-drive models having finished that July, and overlapped by five months with production of the revised V8-250 models which succeeded them.

Minor changes generally paralleled those made to the Mk 2 Jaguars, and were made for the same reasons. 'Chassis' and suspension modifications were almost invariably the same. Unique to the Daimlers, however, was a change very early in the production

The Daimler retained its foglamps when the Jaguars lost theirs in 1967. This is the V8-250, the second-generation model which shared new slimline bumpers with the Jaguar 240 and 340.

run from the original air filter with intake trumpets at the side to a more attractive type with twin forward-facing intakes; quite possibly the change was made for aesthetic reasons.

A strike at the Salisbury company which made Jaguar's axles disrupted supplies after the middle of November 1964, with the result that a number of cars had to be fitted with 4.27:1 axles instead of the 4.55:1 type. Although this change was made purely to keep the assembly lines moving, it proved to be much appreciated, and Jaguar actually standardized the 4.27 axle in mid-May 1965. Its taller ratio gave the Daimler slightly better fuel economy at a slight cost to acceleration, thus giving it a balance of features more generally appreciated by the typical Daimler customer. However, not every Daimler buyer was staid and elderly: demand led Jaguar to offer the option of a limited-slip differential after 1965, and of course the manual gearbox during 1967.

THE V8-250

The compact Daimlers were modified in September 1967 at the same time as the Mk 2 Jaguars became 240 and 340 models. However, the announcement of the Daimler revisions was made a week after the Jaguar announcement, to give Browns Lane two bites of the publicity cherry. Since August 1966, what Jaguar called the XDM2/2 (second-generation XDM2) had existed in prototype form and the first of the new cars was built in July 1967; left-hand-drive examples followed during August.

It was logical that the revised cars should have a three-digit name in line with the revised Jaguars' 240 and 340, and 250 was the obvious choice because of their engine size. However, the cars were actually called V8-250 models, and were badged as such

---

Optional extras for the 2.5-litre V8 models

Ace Turbo wheel trims
Child-proof locks for rear doors
Column-mounted combined ignition
  and starter switch
Laminated windscreen
Limited-slip differential
Lockable fuel filler cap
Power-assisted steering
Radio
Radio aerial (for roof or wing; also
  wing-mounted manually
  retractable type with winding
  handle under dash)
Radio speaker for rear shelf, with
  balance control
Rimbellishers for wheels
Safety belts (front seats only)
Steel sunroof
Sundym tinted glass
Tow-bar
Wing mirrors (standard or Paddy
  Hopkirk sports style)
Wire wheels (in chrome)

---

with the earlier V8 badge alongside a separate '250' on the boot lid.

Even though many of the changes made to the Daimlers paralleled those on the Jaguars, there was one fundamental difference: the Daimlers were not in any sense cheapened. Like the 240 and 340 Jaguars, the V8-250 was given slimmer bumpers and overriders, together with new hubcaps (although these of course had a 'D' on their centre badges). The Rimbellishers remained standard and the Daimlers did not lose their foglamps. As with the Jaguars, metallic paints were deleted from the options list, while new solid colours were added. Inside the cars, reclining front seats were now standard and leather upholstery was still the order of the day, although this now had perforated 'breathing' panels. The heated rear window was also a standard fitment, and the dashboard now had a black Rexine-covered padded top, while padding which matched the interior trim colour was continued around the wooden door cappings in the style pioneered by the 1966 Jaguar 420.

There were mechanical changes, too. Marles Varamatic power-assisted steering replaced the earlier type, an alternator and negative-earth electrical system replaced the dynamo and positive-earth system, and the engine gained twin air filters instead of the single pancake type in order to make maintenance work on the carburettors rather easier.

The standard late-1960s Jaguar wheeltrims wore Daimler centre badges on the V8-250 model.

The Daimler name was moulded into the glass of the reversing lamp.

V8-250 PRODUCTION CHANGES, 1967–1969

The Daimler V8-250 was in production for a fraction over two years, and was never built in large quantities. Overseas sales were in any case minimal, and no more than 105 left-hand-drive cars were built, while fewer than 5,000 right-hand-drive examples came off the lines. After 1968, of course, the Daimler Sovereign version of the new XJ6 creamed off many sales, and production was halted over the summer of 1969. The last left-hand-drive V8-250 was built on 9 July 1969, and the last V8-250 of all a month later on 5 August.

During this short production run, there were no changes of any note. However, Jaguar did specify stronger new pistons during 1968, as there had been service failures, apparently caused by overheating, to which the engine was never subject in the SP250 sports car. As this modification was made so late in the day, it is tempting to assume that the problem only occurred when the engine was used enthusiastically in conjunction with the manual gearbox which had not been available until the previous year. Further changes included a different camshaft, a modified cylinder block and a modified sump.

The Daimler V8 engine was not carried over for any subsequent model and ceased production at the same time as the V8-250s themselves. It was a fine engine which could undoubtedly have been further developed, but there was no room for it in the British Leyland scheme of things. The V8-250 was the only model for which it was being built by 1969, as the SP250 sports car had disappeared some five years earlier, and British Leyland did not want a third V8 model alongside the existing Rover 3.5-litre V8 and forthcoming Triumph 3-litre V8. The cost of production was also an important factor in its demise, because the Daimler engine was very labour-intensive to manufacture.

Daimlers – this is a V8-250 – had a single exhaust pipe on each side of the rear valance.

Optional extras for the V8-250 models

Overdrive
Power-assisted steering
Radio
Radio aerial
Seat belts
Special paint finishes
Wire wheels (in chrome)

THE COMPACT DAIMLERS ON THE ROAD

The Daimler engine made an enormous difference to the character of the compact Jaguar. Whereas the XK-engined models always seemed to have a sporting feel to them, the Daimler always felt much more like a rather old-fashioned luxury car. The relaxed nature of the V8 engine and its refined operation somehow encouraged a more sedate driving style than the Jaguars, and it was hardly surprising that the Daimler was seen as a more sedate car, best suited to the driving style of older customers.

However, the fact was that the Daimler *could* be encouraged to pick up its skirts and fly; it was simply the character of the car which encouraged a more leisurely driving style. Even when equipped with automatic transmission (as the majority were), it would easily out-accelerate a manual 2.4-litre Jaguar – and its top speed was very much higher, too. The later cars with manual gearboxes were even quicker and when fitted with overdrive were considerably more economical than the automatics. The overdrive also ensured that engine revs were less frenetic at high speeds than in the automatic or non-overdrive manual cars and thus actually made a worthwhile con-

tribution to refinement. However, these advantages were largely lost on the traditional Daimler customer, with the result that relatively few cars were sold with the four-speed manual or overdrive options.

Even though the V8 engine was a lot lighter than any of the Jaguar sixes, the Daimler cars still carried just over 57 per cent of their weight over the front wheels. This meant that quite strong understeer was the dominant cornering characteristic, just as in the Jaguars, although the Daimlers were to some extent rather better balanced. Roadholding and ride qualities were otherwise very similar to the Jaguars', and the latter especially was wholly in keeping with what was expected of a compact luxury saloon in the 1960s. In every way, the compact Daimlers were fitting descendants of the Daimler Conquest and Conquest Century models of the 1950s, even though the bloodline had lost its purity.

The fluted number-plate shroud and V8-250 badging leave no doubt about the identity of this car.

Daimler 2.5-litre V8 and V8-250: typical performance figures

	2.5-litre V8	V8-250 (overdrive)
0–60mph	13.5 secs	10.8 secs
0–90mph	32 secs	30.5 secs
Top speed	110mph (177km/h)	112mph (180km/h)
Fuel consumption	16–20mpg (14–18l/100km)	19–25mpg (11–15l/100km)

RIVALS

With the Daimler compacts, Browns Lane once again found a market niche where there was very little competition and the Daimler's keen pricing must have contributed materially to its success. The buyer who wanted real wood and leather in a sophisticated and refined saloon faced a very simple choice: either buy the Daimler or pay very much more for its like from other manufacturers. And indeed, there was nothing on the British market which could have been considered a direct equivalent of the Daimler, at any price.

When the Daimler 2.5-litre V8 saloon was introduced at the 1962 Earls Court Motor Show, it was priced at £1,785 15s 3d, inclusive of Purchase Tax. There was only one car on the market which could be considered a possible competitor, and that was the Citroën DS19 saloon (which actually cost exactly the same). However, the Citroën was no great seller in Britain and its idiosyncratic features were certainly not likely to appeal to the conservative clientele at whom the Daimler was aimed. Other machinery in this price bracket was either sporting and impractical (the Alfa Romeo 1600 Spider at £1,798 2s 9d was hardly a Daimler alternative) or large and lumbering (the Humber Super Snipe Estate Car weighed in at £1,781 12s 9d).

The picture remained much the same in 1964, although Citroën's British factory at Slough had now upgraded the DS19 with wooden dashboard trim and other features designed to give it a more 'British' appeal. A year later, however, the Daimler's price had increased to £1,599 while the Citroën's had been pegged at £1,570 and that of the Humbers had escalated considerably. The Daimler now cost more than a Jaguar 3.8-litre Mk 2 at £1,558, but there was no new direct competition. As it happened, the six-cylinder Rambler saloon had been introduced at the same price, £1,599, but once again that appealed to a quite different sector of the market – and in fact went on to sell only in tiny numbers in Britain.

The Citroëns remained on sale at prices similar to the Daimler's for the next three years, the DS19 at £1,597 still being the Daimler's only real competitor when the V8-250 was announced at a price of £1,616 at the 1967 Earls Court Motor Show. There were still no other serious rivals, and by now the Daimler was by far the most expensive of the compacts from Browns Lane, the Jaguar 340 being a mere £1,442.

By the time of the 1968 Show, however, there was new competition. The V8-engined Rover Three Thousand Five had been introduced that April, and at £1,790 19s 5d represented a formidable threat to the automatic Daimler which was priced at £1,826 15s 0d. Browns Lane did manage to undercut the Rover by offering the new overdrive-equipped Daimler at a bargain £1,785 18s 2d, but the writing was already on the wall. The basic Jaguar XJ6 2.8 could now be bought for £1,797 7s 3d, and the V8-250 now seemed expensive by comparison. It was hardly surprising that the 1968 Show was the compact Daimler's last appearance at Earls Court.

Identification: Daimler 2.5-litre V8 and V8-250

Identification numbers are stamped on a plate in the engine compartment, attached to the right-hand inner wing. These numbers are repeated elsewhere as follows.

Car (chassis, VIN) Number
The car number is stamped in the bonnet catch channel, forward of the radiator header tank, and on the top of the nearside frame member above the rear engine mounting bracket. A typical car number would be 1A3347BW. This breaks down into three elements:

1A	model type code (see below)
3347	serial number (see below)
BW	transmission type (see below)

Model type codes are:

1A	2.5-litre V8
1K	V8-250

Sequences are as follows:

	RHD	LHD
2.5 V8	1001 - 13377	20001 - 20622
V8-250	1001 - 5780	30001 - 30105

Suffixes are:

BW	Borg Warner automatic gearbox
DN	(Laycock) DeNormanville overdrive

Cars fitted with power-assisted steering have a P prefix, eg P1A3347BW.

Engine Number
The engine number is stamped on the side of the cylinder block above the oil filter. On cars built after May 1968 it is stamped on the engine bell-housing on the left-hand side. A typical engine number would be 7A13702. This breaks down into two elements:

7A	engine type identifier (see below)
13702	serial number

Sequences are as follows:

2.5 V8	7A
V8-250	7K

Body Number

On cars built before 1965, the body number is stamped on a small plate attached to the right-hand side of the scuttle, under the bonnet.

On cars built after 1965, the body number is stamped on a small plate attached to the right-hand side of the body behind the rear bumper. (It should not be confused with a similar plate on the left-hand side which gives the Pressed Steel reference number.)

Gearbox Number

The gearbox number on cars with automatic transmission is stamped on a plate attached to the left-hand side of the transmission casing. The gearbox number of manual and overdrive gearboxes is stamped on a small shoulder at the left-hand rear corner of the gearbox and on the rim of the core plug aperture on the top cover.

Annual production breakdown: Daimler V8 saloons

2.5-litre V8

	RHD		LHD		Total
1962	1001 to 1024	(24)	20001 to 20004	(4)	28
1963	1025 to 3342	(2,318)	20005 to 20256	(252)	2,570
1964	3343 to 7161	(3,819)	20257 to 20363	(107)	3,926
1965	7162 to 10400	(3,239)	20364 to 20481	(118)	3,357
1966	10401 to 12496	(2,095)	20482 to 20556	(75)	2,170
1967	12497 to 13377	(881)	20557 to 20622	(66)	947
		12,376		622	12,998

V8-250

	RHD		LHD		Total
1967	1001 to 1847	(847)	30001 to 30042	(42)	889
1968	1848 to 4696	(2,849)	30043 to 30094	(52)	2,901
1969	4697 to 5780	(1,084)	30095 to 30105	(11)	1,095
		4,780		105	4,885

Note: These figures are from the Daimler and Lanchester Owners' Club and do not agree with the Heritage figures.

Daimler 2.5-litre V8 (1961–1967)
Layout
Monocoque bodyshell with front subframe bolted in place. Five-seater saloon, with front engine and rear wheel drive.

Engine
Type	Daimler overhead-valve V8
Block material	Cast iron
Head material	Aluminium alloy
Cylinders	Eight, in vee
Cooling	Water
Bore and stroke	76.2 × 69.85mm
Capacity	2,548cc
Main bearing	Five
Valves	Two per cylinder
Compression ratio	8.2:1
Carburettors	Twin SU HD6
Max. power	140bhp @ 5,800rpm
Max. torque	155lb/ft @ 3,600rpm

Transmission
Automatic models	Torque converter

Internal gearbox ratios
(Three-speed automatic only)
Top	1.00:1
Intermediate	1.45:1
First	2.39:1
Final drive	4.55:1 (to November 1964); 4.27:1 (from November 1964)

Suspension and steering
Front	Independent, wtih wishbones, coil springs and anti-roll bar
Rear	Live axle with radius arms, Panhard rod and semi-elliptic leaf springs
Steering	Recirculating ball, worm-and-nut; power assistance optional
Tyres	6.40 × 15
Wheels	Five-stud type; optional wire-spoke type
Rim width	5in

Brakes
Type	Servo-assisted discs front and rear
Size	Front 11in, rear 11.375in

Dimensions (in/mm)
Track, front	55.0/1,3997
Track, rear	53.375/1,355
Wheelbase	107.375/2,727
Overall length	180.75/4,591
Overall width	66.75/1,695
Overall height	57.75/1,467
Unladen weight	3,046lb/1,382kg

DAIMLER V8-250 (1967–1969)

Layout
Monocoque bodyshell with front subframe bolted in place. Five-seater saloon, with front engine and rear wheel drive.

Engine
Type	Daimler overhead-valve V8
Block material	Cast iron
Head material	Aluminium alloy
Cylinders	Eight, in vee
Cooling	Water
Bore and stroke	76.2 × 69.85mm
Capacity	2,548cc
Main bearings	Five
Valves	Two per cylinder
Compression ratio	8.2:1
Carburettors	Twin SU HD6
Max. power	140bhp @ 5,800rpm
Max. torque	155lb/ft @ 3,600rpm

Transmission
Manual models	Hydraulically operated single dry plate clutch, 10in diameter
Automatic models	Torque converter

Internal gearbox ratios
Option 1   Three-speed automatic
Top	1.00:1
Intermediate	1.21:1
First	1.36:1
Final drive	4.27:1

Option 2   Four-speed manual
Top	1.00:1
Third	1.33:1
Second	1.97:1
First	3.04:1
Final drive	4.27:1

Option 3   Four-speed manual with overdrive
Overdrive	0.77:1
Top	1.00:1
Third	1.33:1
Second	1.97:1
First	3.04:1
Final drive	4.55:1

Suspension and steering

Front	Independent, with wishbones, coil springs and anti-roll bar
Rear	Live axle with radius arms, Panhard rod and semi-elliptic leaf springs
Steering	Recirculating ball, worm-and-nut; power assistance optional
Tyres	6.40 × 15
Wheels	Five-stud disc type; optional wire-spoke type
Rim width	5in

Brakes

Type	Servo-assisted discs front and rear
Size	Front 11in, rear 11.375in

Dimensions (in/mm)

Track, front	55.0/1,397
Track, rear	53.375/1,355
Wheelbase	107.375/2,727
Overall length	180.75/4,591
Overall width	66.75/1,695
Overall height	57.75/1,467
Unladen weight	3,046lb/1,382kg

Colours and trims – Daimler 2.5-litre V8 and V8-250

These cars generally had a rather smaller selection of the colours and trims available on the contemporary Mk 2 and 240/340 Jaguar ranges. The 2.5-litre V8 models were more commonly finished in opalescent (metallic) colours than were their Jaguar contemporaries. As with the Jaguars, it was possible to order non-standard paint and trim colours.

(i) 2.5-litre V8

October 1962 to November 1964
There were six standard paint colours, of which four were metallic finishes. Eight interior trim colours were available.

British Racing Green	with trim in	Beige, Black or Green
Old English White		Black or Red
Opalescent Dark Green		Suede Green or Tan
Opalescent Gunmetal		Red or Tan
Opalescent Silver BlueDark Blue,		Grey, Light Blue or Red
Opalescent Silver Grey		Grey, Red or Tan

Note: A few very early cars, including 1A1001 which was the Earls Court Show car, were finished in Opalescent Maroon. At least one car – 1A1004, also shown at Earls Court – was also finished in Cotswold Blue. Neither of these colours appears to have been standard.

December 1964 to March 1966

There were ten standard paint colours, of which five were metallic finishes. The same eight interior trim colours remained available.

British Racing Green	with trim in	Beige, Black or Green
Indigo Blue		Black, Dark Blue or Red
Old English White		Black or Red
Opalescent Dark Green		Suede Green or Tan
Opalescent Golden Sand		Red or Tan
Opalescent Gunmetal		Red or Tan
Opalescent Silver Blue		Dark Blue, Grey, Light Blue or Red
Opalescent Silver Grey		Grey, Red or Tan
Pale Blue		Black, Dark Blue or Red
Warwick Grey		Black, Dark Blue, Red or Tan

April 1966 to March 1967

Colours and trims remained unchanged except that Black was now listed among the standard colours. There were therefore now eleven standard paints, including five metallics.

Black	with trim in	Beige, Dark Blue orRed
British Racing Green		Beige, Black or Green
Indigo Blue		Black, Dark Blue or Red
Old English White		Black or Red
Opalescent Dark Green		Suede Green or Tan
Opalescent Golden Sand		Red or Tan
Opalescent Gunmetal		Red or Tan
Opalescent Silver Blue		Dark Blue, Grey, LightBlue or Red
Opalescent Silver Grey		Grey, Red or Tan
Pale Blue		Black, Dark Blue or Red
Warwick Grey		Black, Dark Blue, Redor Tan

March 1967 to August 1967

The colour range was reduced to just nine standard colours, of which one was a metallic. Interior trim materials and colours remained as before.

Beige	with trim in	Light Tan, Red, Suede Green or Tan
Black		Grey, Light Tan, Red or Tan
British Racing Green		Beige, Light Tan, Suede Green or Tan
Carmen Red		Beige or Red
Cream		Dark Blue, Light Blue or Red
Dark Blue		Grey, Light Blue or Red
Opalescent Dark Green		Beige, Light Tan, Suede Green or Tan
Warwick Grey		Dark Blue, Light Blue or Tan
Willow Green		Beige, Grey, Light Tan or Suede Green

(ii) V8-250

September 1967 to July 1969
There were six standard exterior colours, none of which were metallics. Four interior trim colours were available. Upholstery was in Ambla, with leather an extra-cost option.

Beige	with trim in	Beige, Black, Blue or Red
Black		Beige, Black, Blue or Red
British Racing Green		Beige or Black
Cream		Beige, Black, Blue or Red
Dark Blue		Beige, Black, Blue or Red
Warwick Grey		Beige, Black, Blue or Red

9 The Compacts in Competition

The compact Jaguars had a major and lasting impact on the competition scene, although their competition heyday was a relatively short one. Their greatest successes were achieved between 1957 (when the 3.4-litre Mk 1s became available) and 1963 (after which the Lotus Cortinas took over from the 3.8-litre Mk 2s as the most successful saloon racers). Most of their successes came on the track, although the early cars also made a name for themselves in rallying.

On the circuits, the Mk 1 Jaguars showed up well right from the beginning, although it took the 3.4-litre engine to give them a serious edge over some of their rivals. However, these early 3.4s were flawed cars which needed further development. With the Mk 2s, Jaguar eliminated most of the problems which had dogged the earlier cars and in the early 1960s the 3.8-litre models completely dominated saloon car racing in Britain as well as scoring notable successes in Germany, Australia and elsewhere.

It was lighter and more nimble machinery which put the 3.8s out of the running for top honours and by the mid-1960s the compact Jaguars were only ever seen on the circuits at club race days. Their popularity at even these events gradually declined, although modified Mk 2s were still to be seen at club days until well into the 1970s. Since then, the arrival of special racing series within the classic car scene has contributed to a revival of their popularity as competition machines.

The Mk 1 cars were also quite successful as rally cars, although they were always handicapped by weight and a certain lack of agility. These drawbacks counted against their Mk 2 descendants much more heavily in the early 1960s as international rallies became very much tougher, and the Mk 2 never did make the grade as a rally car despite some minor successes.

By the time the 240s and 340s became available in 1967, the compacts were no longer considered as serious competition machinery of any sort, and so these cars were not generally associated with racing or rallying when they were new. As for the Daimler models, both 2.5-litre V8 and V8-250, their competition career during their production lifetime was virtually non-existent.

THE WORKS PERIOD, 1955–1956

The compact Jaguars all but missed out on the period when Jaguar ran its own highly successful works team. Launched in the autumn of 1955 but not available in quantity until the beginning of 1956, they made their competition debut during the first months of that year. Promising though this was, they had hardly any chance to follow it up: before the works compacts were able to show their mettle again, Jaguar decided to pull out of competition. The 3.4-litre cars,

A 'works' 2.4-litre Jaguar during its first appearance on the circuits in May 1956. Duncan Hamilton is driving RVC591 in the Daily Express *Production Car Race at Silverstone, and would bring it home in third place. The Mk VII, also a 'works' car, is being driven by Paul Frère.*

which did not become available until 1957, never did race as members of the Jaguar works team - but works-prepared cars did race in the hands of privateers and Jaguar continued for many years to provide advice and assistance to drivers who stood a good chance of upholding the Jaguar name in competitive events.

The works compacts made their competition debut in the RAC Rally, which began on 6 March 1956. This event demanded both tight time schedules in the navigational exercises on the road and speed in the special tests run at a number of racing circuits. The works 2.4 (JWK753) driven by Bill Bleakley and navigated by Ian Hall put up a good performance to take fourth place overall behind the winning Aston Martin, Ian Appleyard's second-placed XK140, and a Morgan. In this position it was both the highest-placed saloon and won the over 2,000cc Production Touring Cars class, which was no small achievement for a com-

pletely untried saloon.

The next appearance of the works 2.4 Jaguars was at the Silverstone Production Car Race in May, when one car (RKV456) was driven by Mike Hawthorn and the second by Duncan Hamilton. Also competing in a 2.4 was Jaguar dealer John Coombs. Hawthorn's car took the lead from the start, but dropped out after only two laps with a broken valve spring; Hamilton, however, brought his car home to a creditable third position.

Just a fortnight later, Paul Frère came a convincing first in the Production Car Race at Spa, in Belgium, driving a works-prepared 2.4. This car had a C-type cylinder head, 2-inch SU carburettors and a close-ratio gearbox, and Frère's win represented the first ever outright win for a compact Jaguar.

That, however, was to be that as far as the works 2.4s were concerned. On 13 October, Jaguar announced that it would no longer field a works team, at least for the present. The reason given was that the company's engineering division was too heavily committed to forthcoming model developments, which was no doubt only partly true. One way or another, no more compact Jaguars would race under the auspices of a Jaguar works team.

PRIVATEERS ON THE TRACK, 1956–1959

Over the next three years, the 2.4-litre Jaguars continued to be popular in both circuit and rally events in the hands of privateers, but the better drivers – and the wealthier ones among the others – switched to the new 3.4-litre cars as soon as they became available in the first quarter of 1957. Little of significance happened for nearly a year after Jaguar's withdrawal from competition, however, mainly because the Suez Crisis and the petrol shortages and rationing which ensued played havoc with the motor sport calendar in Europe. The British Government approved allocations of petrol for some events in April 1957 and things gradually returned to normal.

In the meantime, Jaguar had found the time to prepare three of the new 3.4-litre cars for privateers, and these appeared in the Production Car Race at Silverstone during September. The drivers – all names familiar from the Jaguar works teams of old – were Mike Hawthorn, Duncan Hamilton and Ivor Bueb, who finished first, second and third respectively to win the team prize for Jaguar and start the 3.4's competition career with a flourish. Perhaps almost equally impressive was that fifth place in the race went to Ron Flockhart, who was driving John Coombs' 2.4-litre car.

However, it took a skilful and courageous driver to pilot one of these early 3.4s to victory. Hawthorn's RVC592, Hamilton's

VDU384 and Bueb's VDU385 all suffered from brake fade, a problem which had become apparent during the very first outings of the 2.4-litre cars in 1956. The new disc brakes – by September already a production option – made the compact Jaguars quite a different proposition, and it would probably be no exaggeration to say that, without them, the 3.4 Jaguar would not have gone on to dominate saloon car racing as it did over the next few years. Allied to the Jaguars' notoriously heavy steering, poor braking would have been enough to scare off many a lesser driver.

The 3.4s starred in just one more important event before 1957 drew to a close. Tommy Sopwith and Sir Gawaine Baillie had both bought themselves 3.4-litre Jaguars and at the Brands Hatch Touring Car Race held on Boxing Day, they brought them home in first and second places. Sopwith's first-placed car bore the registration number EN400, and was a car of which the racegoing public was destined to see very much more. During 1958 he and Baillie would continue to delight the crowds with their Jaguars, as would Hawthorn, Bueb and Hamilton.

It was a 1-2-3 victory for the Jaguars of Hamilton, Sopwith and Flockhart at the Silverstone Touring Car Race in 1958, and by now the news about the 3.4 was spreading. So it was that the American sports car champion Walter Hansgen – one of Briggs Cunningham's team – entered a Coombs-prepared 3.4 (TWK287) in the saloon car race held on Grand Prix day at Silverstone that year. Sopwith's Jaguar led until it lost a wheel at about half-distance, when Hansgen inherited the lead and retained it with ease to the end. He was followed past the finishing line by a procession of three more 3.4-litre Jaguars, driven by Baillie, Crawley and Uren.

That year was a great one for Tommy Sopwith, who raced as team leader for

Equipe Endeavour, and allowed him to end his distinguished racing career on a high note. At Crystal Palace, where a saloon car event was held for the first time during a BRSCC event, he took first place and fastest lap honours in his 3.4 and was followed over the line by Sir Gawaine Baillie and Jeff Uren, both also in 3.4 Jaguars. At Brands Hatch in October he won again, and at Snetterton later that month he took his 3.4 to the chequered flag for the last time.

With Sopwith no longer in the running, and Hawthorn tragically killed at the wheel of his 3.4-litre Jaguar on the road early in the new year, 1959 was bound to be different. Moreover, it was to be the final year of production for the original compact Jaguars; but they were able to pave the way splendidly for their Mk 2 successors by continuing their dominance of saloon car events.

At Equipe Endeavour, Ivor Bueb took over from Tommy Sopwith as team leader, and on the tracks he was also to inherit

---

Specification: Mike Hawthorn's 1957 3.4 (VDU881)

Engine   2in SU carburettors
9:1 compression pistons
Special exhaust with twin
    tail pipes

Transmission
Competition clutch
Axle ratio 4.05:1

Suspension
Rear track increased by
    2in with special wheels
Stronger front springs
Additional leaf in rear
    springs
Competition dampers all
    round

Brakes   Discs on all four wheels,
with servo and special
Mintex pads

Sopwith's mantle. Bueb's 3.4, bearing the fictional registration plate IVA400, took first place in the Production Car races at Silverstone, Aintree and Goodwood, in each case leaving the second place to Roy Salvadori in the Coombs-prepared 3.4, 287JPK, and the third place to Sir Gawaine Baillie in another 3.4, UXD400. And at Silverstone, the next three places were also taken by compact Jaguars, fourth and fifth going to Dick Protheroe and Dixon in 3.4s and sixth to Peter Bland in a 2.4-litre car. Finally, over in the USA where the 3.4-litre Jaguar was enjoying huge popularity, Walter Hansgen managed to persuade Jaguar to prepare him an example which he then took to victory in the US Grand Prix compact sedan race.

PRIVATEERS IN RALLYING, 1956–1959

There is little doubt that the brothers Don and Erle Morley were the stars of Jaguar rallying in the late 1950s, although they were far from being the only team to take honours with the compact saloons. In 1957, 1958 and 1959, they made the Tulip Rally their own, driving first a 2.4-litre and then a 3.4-litre Jaguar and working their way up from third in class, through a class win and eighth overall, to outright victory. Both the 2.4, which they drove in the 1957 and 1958 events, and the 3.4 they had for 1959 wore the same registration number, DJM400.

That 3.4-litre car remained in everyday use for a further six years, but it was never rallied again. Impressed by the brothers' winning performance in the 1959 Tulip Rally, Marcus Chambers of the BMC Competitions Department made them an offer they were more than happy to accept, and thereafter their rallying career was pursued at the wheel of an Austin Healey 3000.

One of the most famous competition 3.4-litre Mk 1s was Mike Hawthorn's car, VDU881. It is just possible to tell in this picture that the rear track was wider than standard.

Sir Gawaine Baillie's wire-wheeled 3.4-litre Mk 1 leans into a bend during the saloon car race at Brands Hatch on Boxing Day, 1957. UXO400 later appeared on the tracks in different colours.

The 1957 rallying season was truncated somewhat by the Suez Crisis – that year's Monte was cancelled – and the compact Jaguars scored no more rally successes that year. However, 1958 showed more promise. The large number of hopefuls who entered that year's Monte in Jaguars was a clear demonstration of the respect in which the car was by then held, but the results were unspectacular. The highest-placed Jaguar was the 3.4 of Carris and Béziers, which was placed second in its class but no higher than twenty-fourth in the overall classification. The RAC, Acropolis, Scottish and Liège–Rome–Liège Rallies all produced class wins for the compact Jaguars, but they were unable to return greater honours and by the end of the season it was beginning to look as if the cars would not be able to duplicate their circuit successes in international rally events.

Yet 1959 produced its share of victories.

Not only did the Morley brothers take first overall in the Tulip Rally, but Nano da Silva Ramos drove his 3.4 to first place in the Tour de France. In the Monte and the Scottish Rally that year, compact Jaguars again recorded class wins, and in the minor Sestrières Rally, the German team of Plaut and Heinemann took a second in class with their 3.4.

Undeniably, however, the 2.4-litre and 3.4-litre Jaguars were much better suited to track events than to the mixture of road runs and special stages which made up the typical rally of the late 1950s. Their handicap was never a lack of speed, and nor did they lack the robustness of the winning cars. The problem seems to have been more associated with excessive weight and a consequent lack of agility. Nevertheless, 1959's two overall wins showed that the Jaguars could be competitive, and especially so in the right hands.

Don and Erle Morley won the 1957 Tulip Rally with DJM400, a 3.4-litre car which was also used for everyday transport.

PRIVATEERS AND THE MK 2 – CIRCUIT RACING, 1960–1964

From the moment the 3.8-litre Mk 2 was announced in 1959, saloon racing enthusiasts knew it was the car they wanted. The older 3.4-litre cars already enjoyed a formidable reputation, and here was a car with even more power and torque, plus vital improvements in handling and roadholding. The drivers could hardly wait to get their hands on it.

Nor did the car disappoint them. The 3.8-litre Jaguar first appeared on the circuits during the 1960 racing season, and in that year and the following one it proved all but unbeatable. Its domination of saloon car racing in Europe continued throughout 1962 and 1963, but the competition had by this time become tougher. The first big American racing saloons had reached British circuits during 1961, when the Chevrolet Impalas had given the 3.8s a run for their money. In May 1962 a 3.8 was beaten on the tracks for the first time by a Chevrolet (in fact a Chevy II model), and during 1963 the Jaguars often had to give best to the thundering 7-litre Ford Galaxies driven by former 3.8 Jaguar drivers Jack Sears, Peter Jopp and Sir Gawaine Baillie, among others. By 1964 it was all over. The new Ford Lotus Cortinas swept the field, leaving the Jaguars trailing in their wake.

Yet in those four years, the 3.8-litre Jaguars had created a legend. They were highly respected by competitions drivers, and it was not uncommon to see starting grids very nearly full of 3.8s, or to see two, three, or even four of these cars among the first five places. They succeeded mainly because they were both fast and durable, and even when the big American cars started to leave them behind on the straights they were usually able to catch up on the corners because of their excellent handling and roadholding. In the end, it was weight which was their undoing. During their heyday, they were notoriously heavy on tyres (one set might last no longer than a single race), and when the much lighter and more nimble Lotus Cortinas arrived, the 3.8s were simply outclassed.

Although dozens of individuals raced Mk 2 Jaguars in the early 1960s, the major successes went to the racing teams which could employ top-class drivers. The two leading teams were Equipe Endeavour and Coombs; but some individuals also did remarkably well and the names which stand out are those of Sir Gawaine Baillie and Peter Lindner, the German Jaguar dealer who managed to secure factory support and put together a team to contest the new European Touring Car Championship in 1963.

Equipe Endeavour had already established a name for itself with the 3.4-litre Mk 1 cars, and proceeded to maintain its reputation with 3.8-litre Mk 2s. Its most famous car was registered as JAG400, and its regular driver for the 1960 season was Jack Sears; Stirling Moss also put in a single appearance that season, driving JAG400. For 1961 Mike Parkes was the team driver and Graham Hill guested, while 1962 saw Parkes again at Equipe Endeavour and Jack Sears returning to the fold. However, the team did not show for 1963.

The first appearance of the Mk 2 in competition was at the Goodwood meeting on Easter Monday, 1960. Jack Sears put up a fierce fight in the Equipe Endeavour car, but was eventually placed third behind Roy Salvadori in the Coombs team car, and both conceded victory to Stirling Moss in an Aston Martin DB4. However, Moss himself took over JAG400 for the Silverstone International Trophy Race in May, and carried off second place, again behind Salvadori in the Coombs car. JAG400 raced again at Silverstone in July, taking a second place in the Touring Car race when driven

Jack Sears driving the Equipe Endeavour car, JAG400, at the Aintree 200 saloon car race meeting in 1961. He came second.

by Jack Sears and then a further second place in Mike Parkes' hands in the Production Cars event.

Equipe Endeavour showed well at the May 1961 Silverstone meeting, too. Mike Parkes managed second place while the race was won by Graham Hill, driving a second Equipe Endeavour car. Parkes was Jack Sears' co-driver when the Jaguar raced at the Lombard Trophy meeting at Snetterton and the pair would have won if they had not run out of petrol on the very last lap while leading the race! Then it was Parkes once again who represented Equipe Endeavour in the Circuit of Ireland road race, when he carried off a class win.

Both Parkes and Sears entered Jaguars in the races supporting the British Grand Prix at Aintree in 1962 and Sears took first place. He also raced in the Oulton Park Trophy, but without result. However, Parkes won at Snetterton and Brands Hatch and Sears pulled off a second place at Crystal Palace in June. But the best result by Equipe Endeavour that season was in

the six-hour endurance race sponsored by *The Motor* magazine and held at Brands Hatch in October. This was the first long-distance saloon car event to be held in Britain and resulted in a first place for Mike Parkes and his co-driver Jimmy Blumer in JAG400.

Like Equipe Endeavour, the Coombs team had also made its name racing Mk 1 Jaguars in the late 1950s. Coombs raced several modified 3.8-litre Mk 2s, the best-known being registered as 6PPF, BUY1 and BUY12, which all raced in the Coombs team colour of Pearl Grey. Roy Salvadori was the team's main driver for 1960 and 1961, although Colin Chapman (of Lotus Cars) also put in one appearance at the wheel of a Coombs car during 1960. For 1962 Salvadori was joined by Graham Hill, who had previously driven 3.8s for Team Speedwell, but for 1963 the Coombs team turned its attentions elsewhere.

The 1960 season began with promise as Salvadori came second with 6PPF to Moss's Aston at the Goodwood meeting on Easter

4576NK was a Coombs-modified 3.4-litre Mk 2, and it is seen here in the hands of P. J. Woodroffe at Silverstone on 9 September 1961. The car was later converted to run a 3.8-litre engine.

A typical scene at Goodwood in the early 1960s, with no fewer than seven Mk 2 Jaguars among the ten cars visible.

Monday. At Silverstone in May, he won the International Trophy race; but it was Colin Chapman who piloted 6PPF to victory at the races supporting the British Grand Prix at Silverstone in July. The Coombs cars put up several good fights during 1961, but this was a less successful season for them. In 1962 they bounced back, however, now with Graham Hill in the team. Hill secured first places at Oulton Park, Aintree, Goodwood, Silverstone, Mallory Park and Snetterton to become that season's outstanding Jaguar saloon driver. Salvadori also pulled in some good results, taking BUY12 to first place at Crystal Palace in June, losing nobly to the big American cars at the Oulton Park Trophy Race, but coming in second behind Charles Kelsey's Chevy II at the Brands Hatch meeting in May.

Sir Gawaine Baillie was another driver who had tasted success with the Mk 1 3.4-litre cars, and in the early 1960s he campaigned his new 3.8, GB448, to good effect. To him went the honour of the first outright win by a Mk 2 Jaguar anywhere, at Snetterton during 1960. That year he also took a first in class at Oulton Park, came third in the May meeting at Aintree and was placed fourth in the International Trophy Race at Silverstone that month – behind the 3.8s of Salvadori, Moss and Hill.

During 1961 Baillie continued to turn in some entertaining performances with the 3.8 and was usually well up with the race leaders, though outright victory came his way only once. That was at the Lombard Trophy Race at Snetterton, when a last-lap failure by the leading Equipe Endeavour Jaguar allowed him to cross the finish line first. For 1962 his performance was much the same, embracing a fourth place at Crystal Palace in June, another fourth place in the Oulton Park Trophy Race, and a third behind Salvadori and the winning Chevy II at Brands Hatch in May.

Peter Lindner's main contribution to the racing history of the 3.8 Jaguars was in long-distance endurance racing. He had raced in Jaguars during the later 1950s in his native Germany, but after teaming up with Peter Nöcker he decided to enter a 3.4-litre Mk 2 for the first-ever endurance race to be held at the Nürburgring in 1961. Despite suffering serious clutch trouble and a broken steering column mounting, the Lindner/Nöcker Jaguar crossed the line first – a very clear indication of what was to come. Indeed, Lindner went on to win every race he entered in 1961, and that year became combined German National GT and Touring Car Champion.

Lindner went on to repeat his success with Jaguars in 1962. With Hans-Joachim Walter in the co-driver's seat, he won that year's Nürburgring 12-hour Race, and then came second with Nöcker in the Brands Hatch 6-hour Endurance Race. For 1963, however, things became much more serious. The endurance races had been grouped together to form the new European Touring Car Championship (ETTC), and Lindner was determined to do well. To help him in his aim, he sought assistance from Browns Lane.

That year, the Lindner/Nöcker 3.8 stormed to a last-minute victory at the Nürburgring 12-hour Race after being held up by 37 minutes for repairs to its Panhard rod mounting. It was second in the Brands Hatch 6-hour Endurance Race, and then at Zolder in Belgium, Lindner crashed early on. Nöcker, driving another car, went on to win; and for the remaining races of the 1963 European Touring Car Championship, the two Jaguar drivers co-operated so that (under the points system then in operation), Nöcker had the distinction of becoming the first-ever European Touring Car Champion. The result was a major coup for Jaguar, particularly as some of the most telling victories had been scored against their arch-rivals in Germany, Mercedes-Benz.

Lindner and Nöcker with their Mk 2 at the 1962 Nürburgring 12-hour Race.

THE MK2 GT

Jaguar lost no time in capitalizing on the 3.8-litre car's success in saloon racing, and as early as 1961 there was a proposal to offer for sale a 'Mk 2 GT' model, which would have been nothing short of a road-going racer. According to Peter Wilson, who wrote about his time with the Jaguar Competitions Department in the July 1985 issue of *Thoroughbred and Classic Cars* magazine:

A single car … was roughly assembled. The specification incorporated many features of the racing version, including revised sus-

pension, wide offset wire wheels, increased fuel tankage (achieved by mounting the spare wheel in the boot and fitting a circular tank within the spare wheel well), high ratio steering and individual competition type bucket seats.

The 3.8-litre engine would have had three 2in SU carburettors (as used in the production E-type) and standard power output would therefore presumably have been the E-type's 265bhp at 5500rpm. However, remembered Wilson, 'it was decided at a fairly early stage not to continue with the project and the car was returned to standard.'

Specification: 1962 Equipe Endeavour 3.8 (JAG 400)

Engine	2in SU carburettors, without air cleaners
	Gas-flowed and balanced
	9:1 compression
	Special oil breathers
	Unsilenced dual exhaust system
Transmission	Special gearbox oil breather
	Special oil breather for rear axle
Suspension	Stiffened suspension
	High-geared steering
	7.00 x 15 Dunlop racing tyres
Other	Perspex rear and fixed perspex side windows (standard glass and winder in driver's door)
	Lightweight battery
	Trim, headlining, carpets, sound insulation and draught-excluders removed
	Passenger side facia removed
	Heater removed
Performance	0–90mph in 16.7 seconds

PRIVATEERS AND THE MK 2 – RALLYING

Although 3.8-litre Jaguars were entered for almost every major rally in the early 1960s, the optimism of their crews was rarely rewarded with good results. The Mk 2 was nowhere near as good a rally car as it was a track racer, although over the years it was well-placed in a number of events.

The best result during 1960 was a fourth overall and class win in the RAC Rally, achieved by Jack Sears and Willy Cave in a 3.8. José Behra and René Richard won the Touring Car Class and a Coupe des Alpes in that year's Alpine Rally, which also saw Mike Parkes and Geoff Howarth placed fifth overall and third in class in their 3.8. Bernard Consten and Jacques Renal won their class in the Tour de France by a small margin from Peter Jopp and Sir Gawaine Baillie in another 3.8, while Boardman and Whitworth won their class and came eleventh overall in the Tulip Rally. Altogether less successful were the Jaguar entries for the Monte Carlo Rally, however, an event which never did prove kind to the Mk 2s.

During 1961 the Jaguars were once again limited to class wins. Sir Gawaine Baillie and Peter Jopp shared a car again on the Alpine Rally to record one of them, and Bernard Consten won his class for the second year running on the Tour de France.

Parkes and Howarth storm through a French village on the 1960 Tulip Rally in their 3.8-litre Mk 2.

The drivers this time are Gatsonides and Steunebrink, trying their luck with a left-hand-drive 3.8 on the 1960 Tulip Rally.

Other Jaguars took second, third and fourth places behind him. In the RAC Rally and the Monte, however, there were no Jaguar results of any sort, even though 3.8s were among the cars which completed both events.

The picture was similar in 1962. Consten won his class for the third year running in the Tour de France and Jaguars took the next four places in the class as well. Otherwise, it was already clear that the Mk 2s were not proving to be good rally cars. For 1963 results were steady: the Tour de France was again the Jaguars' best show-

ing, Consten again winning the Touring Car category while Annie Soisbault and Louisette Texier claimed second in class with their Mk 2. In the Tulip Rally, Jaguars came second and third in their class, driven by Lundberg with Lindstrom and John Sprinzel with Barry Hughes respectively.

By 1964, however, things had begun to slide. Bernard Consten managed only third place on the Tour de France while Louisette Texier and Marie-Louise Mermod won the Ladies' Award in the Touring Car Class. After that, very little was heard of the rallying Mk 2s.

The Monza record car

The initiative for an attack on the international long-distance driving records during 1963 seems to have come from the oil company Castrol, who secured Jaguar's agreement to use a modified 3.8-litre Mk 2. No doubt Jaguar saw in this record attempt the possibility of valuable publicity to offset the cars' increasing vulnerability to American opposition in saloon car racing.

The original plan was to take as many records as possible over a period of seven days and to that end the Monza racetrack in Italy with its banked circuit was booked at the beginning of March. However, things did not run smoothly. The 3.8 twice suffered damage around the area of the Panhard rod mounting on the rear axle tube and eventually the run had to be aborted while the axle was replaced. As time was running out because the circuit was booked by another team from the middle of the following week, the Castrol-Jaguar team were then forced to limit the number of records they were attempting to break.

Nevertheless, the run was successful. By the time it was over, the car had taken no fewer than four International Class C records, as follows:

10,000 miles (16,100km)	at 106.58mph (171.59km/h) average
15,000km	at 106.61mph (171.64km/h) average
Three days	at 107.02mph (172.3km/h)
Four days	at 106.62mph (171.66km/h)

The actual car used for the record runs was a silver-grey 3.8 Mk 2 with wire wheels, registered 7116VC and prepared for the event by Jaguar. The interior was stripped out to competitions standard and a third windscreen wiper (mounted centrally above the screen) and large spotlamps were added. Mechanical changes included a high 2.93:1 axle and an XK-type exhaust, while the overdrive was locked out to reduce the risk of failure at high speed.

After the Monza event, the car was driven to Geneva, where it was displayed on the Jaguar stand at the 1963 Motor Show.

AFTER THE GLORY – CLASSIC RACING

Even after the Mk 2s had become a spent force in the front line of circuit racing, examples continued to turn up at club events. During the early 1970s many Mk 2s were modified to take the wide wheels and tyres then newly allowed in circuit racing and they continued to give a good account of themselves.

In due course, the growing interest in classic cars during the 1970s led to the establishment of a racing series for older cars, the Pre-'57 Classic Saloon Championship. However, the cut-off date of this series denied access to all the compact Jaguars except for the very early 2.4-litre models, which were hardly competitive. This situation continued until the early 1980s, when the Jaguar Drivers' Club in Britain capitalized on the enthusiasm for Mk 2s and established its own championship. The first events held in 1982, proved so successful that the JDC organized a full Inter-Area Challenge Series for subsequent years.

That series has remained well-supported and popular, and today gives Jaguar enthusiasts a chance to experience the excitement of saloon car racing as it was in the early 1960s – not only as spectators, but as drivers too.

Monza, 1963, and a Mk 2 on the banked circuit where it established new long-distance records. Note the additional windscreen wiper above the screen, and the large auxiliary lamps for night driving.

Two well-known Mk 2 competition cars storm uphill at Brands Hatch.

Specification:Benjamin Sill's 3.8 Club Racer (BAR 883 F)

Engine	2in SU carburettors
	Lightened flywheel
	Balanced
	Gas-flowed head
	Big-bore exhaust
	203bhp at the wheels
Suspension	Lowered suspension
	Uprated springs
	Competition dampers
Brakes	Ventilated front discs with four-pot
	callipers
Performance	0–100mph in 18 seconds
	140mph (225km/h) maximum (estimated)

Benjamin Sill's car is a 1967 340 into which a 3.8-litre Mk 2 engine has been fitted for competition purposes. It has raced both in Britain and abroad and has achieved several class wins in the pre-1968 Jaguar Racing Series.

10 The Compact Jaguars and Daimlers Today

Like all cars which have ceased to be fashion accessories or status symbols, the compact Jaguars and Daimlers entered a period of declining popularity when they went out of production at the end of the 1960s. Prices fell, examples bought cheaply suffered from neglect and abuse, and the cars' high fuel consumption became a liability after the first oil crisis of 1973–1974. By the mid-1970s, many of these once-proud cars had become little more than old bangers, driven until they dropped by unappreciative owners. The scruffiest examples ended their days at banger racing events, smashing into other cars until they could no longer be driven.

However, cars of this calibre never go unloved for long. As early as 1978 *Thoroughbred and Classic Cars* magazine thought the time was right to publish a feature on buying a compact Jaguar and on the pitfalls of ownership. Gradually, despite a second hike in the cost of petrol during 1979, the cars attained what is nowadays called classic status: in other words, they were acknowledged as an important design of their period and as a car which old-car enthusiasts still wanted to own and enjoy. The support industry of spares suppliers, restorers and parts remanufacturers grew to serve this renewed interest and by the end of the 1980s the Mk 2 in particular had become one of the most appreciated classics of the 1960s. During the boom period at the turn of the decade, excellent original and top-quality restored cars were changing hands for ridiculously large sums of money.

The classic-car boom collapsed as the recession arrived in the early 1990s, but the interest in Jaguar's compacts did not recede. They remained among the most popular and sought-after classics and those companies which had sprung up during the boom to update them with modern components continued to thrive. Today's owners of a Jaguar or Daimler compact can rest secure in the knowledge that they share an interest with thousands of others, and that there will be parts and expertise around to assist in keeping a treasured car in pristine condition for years to come.

BUYING – THE CHOICE

There is no shortage of choice when it comes to buying a compact Jaguar or Daimler today. Of the pre-1959 cars, there were two basic engine variants, the 2.4-litre and 3.4-litre. With the Mk 2 Jaguars, the addition of the 3.8-litre engine expanded that choice to three. The 3.8-litre engine disappeared again in 1967, leaving just two variants of the run-out models. Then there were pre-1967 and post-1967 versions of the Daimler. All these add up to a total of nine variants, even before the complications of automatic and overdrive transmission options are considered. Add in rarities like the 3.8-litre 340 and the Coombs-modified

Few compact Jaguars have survived with boot floors as good as this one. There will usually be at least some corrosion in the area of the damper mountings.

cars, and it is clear that there is a very wide range to choose from.

Most prospective owners probably have a favourite model, probably chosen for reasons such as performance, preference for styling of a particular vintage, running costs and purchase cost. However, others may have little preference one way or the other, and would be content simply to own a representative example in good condition. This latter is actually a more sensible approach to ownership, as the cost of restoring a car which is not in good condition can

easily exceed the cost of buying one which is. However, buyers faced with a choice of two or three different models in similar condition at similar prices might need a little guidance, so the next few hundred words are intended to offer some useful pointers.

Generally speaking, Mk 2 (and 240/340) models are a better buy than the pre-1959 cars. They handle better, are generally thought to be better-looking and to have more attractive interiors, and are better supported in terms of parts and expertise. All of this makes them easier to sell on if

A common problem on Mk 2 and 240/340 models is corrosion around the sidelight housings on the front wings. The beginnings of trouble are just visible in this picture.

necessary. The pre-1959 cars are much more of a specialist interest and have survived in very much smaller numbers. They have a very distinctive character of their own, but most owners would admit that they are less suitable for regular use in modern traffic conditions than the later cars. Post-1967 models are seen as less desirable than the Mk 2 proper, mainly because of their 'cheaper' specifications. This affects prices and the ease with which such cars can be sold on, but a 240, 340 or Daimler V8-250 can nevertheless be a very worthwhile classic to own.

Among the Mk 2s, the most desirable cars in theory (and therefore the most expensive) are 3.8-litre models with wire wheels and overdrive, preferably also with the later all-synchromesh transmission and power-assisted steering. However, the truth of the matter is that there are very few occasions when the extra performance of the 3.8-litre engine can be exploited to the full; in the real world, a 3.4-litre car is every bit as usable on today's roads. And even the 2.4-litre and Daimler models are quite fast enough for modern traffic conditions, although they cannot be rated as high-performance cars alongside even the more mundane of modern saloons. Slowest of the bunch, inevitably, is a 2.4-litre Jaguar with automatic transmission; but it has other qualities of refinement and smoothness which have their own appeal.

Some buyers, of course, will be attracted to the compact Jaguars purely because of

It takes hours of skilled work to get a Mk 2 bodyshell back to this condition. This example was seen at the premises of Vicarage, who specialize in Mk 2 restoration.

their eligibility for classic racing. Quite obviously, 3.8-litre engines and overdrive transmissions are the best of the available options, while the early drum-braked cars and all pre-1959 models with their narrow-track rear axles would make poor choices. Those who want a car for classic racing will generally be less interested in the cosmetic condition of any vehicle offered for sale than in its structural and mechanical soundness. Similarly, non-original features (i.e. those which could not have been specified when the car was new) will be of little concern unless they affect the car's eligibility for racing.

However, anyone who wants to buy one of these classic Jaguars or Daimlers needs to inspect a potential purchase very thoroughly indeed. The next sections of this chapter are designed to give guidelines for such an

This sort of Mk 2 used to be much more common than it is today. A 1961 2.4 Automatic, it cost its owner £20 towards the end of the 1970s! Red primer covers up a few blemishes, the wheel spats and foglamps are missing, and the car needs a lot of general tidying but nothing too difficult. The real concern, however, is what the bodyshell is like underneath.

inspection. They are laid out so that all checks from a particular vantage point can be carried out simultaneously.

Before starting an inspection, however, it is advisable to be aware of a few fundamental points. The first is that the condition of a car's bodyshell is the most important criterion when buying. This bodyshell is a monocoque and depends for its strength on the soundness of certain heavily stressed areas. Some of these areas are particularly prone to corrosion, and the combination of rust with stress invariably leads sooner or later to structural failure. Repairs are equally invariably expensive if they are done properly.

The second point to remember is that the cost of proper structural repairs has persuaded many owners to 'bodge' their cars. Sometimes these substandard repairs can be hard to detect, but sooner or later they will reveal themselves. A compact Jaguar or Daimler should always be viewed with a certain amount of suspicion that repairs of this kind are lurking somewhere. It will be a good and well-kept car which has never suffered budget repairs at some time.

The third point is that a properly maintained Jaguar is normally a thoroughly reliable vehicle. Mechanical components last for a very long time and any signs of unreliability may be an indication that a seller has not kept his car up to scratch. In such cases, the best thing to do is to take even greater care over an inspection.

Lastly, most things on most varieties of compact Jaguar can now be replaced, rebuilt or reproduced. However, all work costs money and it is never cheap to buy parts for any of these cars or to get any major work done on them. For that reason, it is best to avoid any car which needs a lot of work to bring it up to respectable condition (unless you have the inclination and the ability to do that work yourself). Far better is to buy the very best car you can

afford and then enjoy using it rather than spending time and money on repairs. Never rush into buying a compact Jaguar or Daimler: there are just too many traps for the unwary.

OUTSIDE THE CAR

The quality of panel fit and finish on these cars when they were new was excellent, so have an initial walk around a car to check such things as panel gaps and the general fit of the panels. Anything which does not look right is likely to be the result of poor repair work, and at worst could be a pointer to hidden structural problems. Make a mental note to take a closer look. As you go, look also for damaged or missing chrome trim strips. It is hard to find replacements in good condition and the originals are made of a soft metal called Mazak which cannot be rechromed.

At the same time, check that the car sits all-square and does not lean to one side. If it sits low at the front, suspect tired coil springs and again make a note to check later. If it sits low at the back, the cause might be tired springs but might also be the partial collapse of their notoriously rust-prone mountings. Again, check more thoroughly later.

The next stage is to look for rust in the outer panels. All too often, this will be readily apparent; on other cars, however, it may be incipient or may have been hastily disguised. At the front of the car, the valance panel behind the bumper is vulnerable, but need not cause too much worry as it is not structural and can be fairly easily replaced or repaired. Bonnet panels should give no cause for concern – but beware of ripples or a poor fit which might suggest half-repaired accident damage.

Your main area of concern should be the front wings, which rust very badly in a number of places. Remanufactured items are available, but are very expensive. More localized corrosion can often be cut out and the damage can be made good with one of the pre-formed repair sections available through specialists. However, even this sort of operation is not cheap, and it does demand a high level of skill if the repair is not to be visible. For all these reasons, therefore, examine the wings carefully.

The usual problem areas include the metal around the sidelights (on pre-1959 cars) or indicators (on later models) in the fronts of the wings, and around the sidelight housings on top of the wings in post-1959 models. Bubbles under the paintwork are usually the first sign of trouble, but in the case of the sidelight housings on top of the wings, look also for the weld seam around them beginning to show through.

Mud and road debris build up under the wings and form a wet poultice which sets up further corrosion. Rust then appears in the nose of the wing, ahead of the wheelarch, around the wheelarch lip, behind the wheelarch and at the lower trailing edge of the wing. Failure of the rubber sealing strip at the back edge of the wing also causes water to sit against the metal and set up corrosion.

Moving further backwards, check for rust in the door bottoms. This is usually caused by blocked drain holes in the bottoms of the frames, which have allowed water to sit against the inner surface of the door skin. Damaged or poorly seating sealing rubbers around the windows simply encourage the problem by allowing more water to get inside the door. Replacement door skins can be bought, but are best fitted by an expert. The chrome on the door handles may well be past its best, but fortunately the compact saloons shared this component with other Jaguar saloons and replacements are not too hard to find. Rechroming is not possible, however, as the handles are made of Mazak.

Open the doors, too, and inspect the seal-ing rubbers; often these will have perished with age and they may have deteriorated to a sponge-like consistency which allows them to retain water and set up rusting in the adjacent metal. Doors should close easily: be suspicious of any which do not and try to discover the cause of the difficulty.

Underneath the doors, the outer sills will often show signs of rust. They are not structural panels and can be fairly simply repaired or replaced. However, beware of oversills, which were a cheap way of repairing the damage. These shaped sills were designed to be welded over the original panels and to save the chore of cutting away the old metal, but of course they also hide from view the corrosion which is continuing behind them!

Rust in the lower trailing edges of the rear wings is usually easy to spot, but it is important also to check the area around the spats. Between spat and wheelarch runs a sealing strip which can deteriorate and hold water against both wing and spat and can initiate corrosion. The spats themselves often rust, too. Replacement panels can be had for the post-1959 cars, but the full spats for early 2.4 models are not available off the shelf and will have to be hand-fabricated, which makes them expensive.

Lastly, check the bottom edge of the boot lid for rust (caused by water getting past a perished rubber seal), which can be awkward to cut out and repair neatly. Then examine the rear valance under the bumper, which gets bombarded with mud and stones thrown up by the wheels and may have started to rust through from the inside. Problems often show up first around the bumper mounting rubbers.

INSIDE THE CAR

In an ideal world, the interior would have that delightful smell of nicely aged leather;

in the real world, it is more likely to smell dank and musty. As the water leaks which cause this smell also ruin carpets, woodwork, door trim and headlinings, be prepared to find some horrors.

Most of the water leaks will probably come from around the windscreen and rear window, where the rubber seals will have dried out with age. Check the headlining for signs of damage in these areas – other damage, such as rips and discoloration, will be more readily apparent – and remember that refurbishment will not be cheap. Replacement headlinings can be bought, but there is no point in fitting a replacement until the water leak has been cured, and that will

mean removing the windscreen or rear window and fitting it together again with a new rubber seal. Headlinings are easier to replace than they might look, although the job does present some difficulties on those models with recessed sun visors.

The figured wood trim goes dull, cracks and can look very down at heel, but undamaged pieces can usually be restored quite simply with a coat of varnish. Specialists can also fettle a car's wood trim and bring it back to as-new condition, but the job is not cheap. Remember that there are no fewer than twenty-four pieces of wood trim inside a Mk 2! Door trims can also deteriorate, particularly if water has attacked their backing

The condition of this Daimler dashboard is not untypical of an abandoned restoration project. Although plenty of work is needed, nothing is beyond hope.

panels from behind. Their heat-moulded seams are impossible to repair or copy at home, but complete remanufactured trims are available through the specialists.

The leather upholstery is one of the cars' many charms and generally wears well. Discoloration can be dealt with quite simply with a re-colouring kit, but tears and other damage need more careful attention. Complete retrims in original-quality leather are frighteningly expensive, but kits to suit the Mk 2's seats are available. Owners of pre-1959 cars and the later Daimlers with perforated leather seat panels are not so lucky, however, and for them any major upholstery renovation will be very expensive. The Ambla interiors in the post-1967 Jaguars actually wear very well and for that reason deserve more respect than they are usually given.

Carpets, particularly in the front footwells, often show signs of wear or of water damage. Fortunately, they are not expensive, and remanufactured items to original specification can be bought off the shelf from specialists. However, it is worth remembering that there are several different types of carpet for these cars, as well as different colours: make sure you order the right type if you buy a replacement set.

There is also one very important area of the interior to check, and that is the seat pan under the rear seat. To get at it, you will have to remove the rear seat cushion, so do seek the owner's permission! However, the rear seat pan is directly above the most highly stressed area of the bodyshell, where the rear springs and suspension arms are mounted. Serious rust, especially in the corners of the seat pan, should ring alarm bells. Check the whole area again when inside the boot and when under the car, but do not be tempted to take on any car which has serious problems here: repairs will be astronomically expensive, if they are feasible at all.

UNDER THE BONNET

There is more to look at under the bonnet than just the engine and its ancillaries! Take a careful look at the inner wing panels, particularly at the back around the bonnet hinges, where serious rust damage can be difficult to repair. It is also worth remembering that the acid from a leaking battery can cause bad corrosion in the bulkhead and that this corrosion is usually concealed from view when the battery is in place. The problem is not as uncommon as it may sound.

The general appearance of an engine can provide helpful clues about its condition and about the sort of maintenance attention it has received. However, steam-cleaning can remove much evidence of neglect and oil leaks and so a suspiciously clean engine should be regarded with caution!

All the Jaguar engines are robust power units which should cover 100,000 miles (160,000km) before needing a major overhaul. However, they are very expensive to rebuild, and you should therefore be on the look-out for evidence of excessive wear. This will come in the form of bad oil leaks, low oil pressure, excessive oil consumption and timing chain clatter. Also worth checking is whether the cooling system is filled with anti-freeze or a corrosion inhibitor; plain water will cause the waterways in the aluminium alloy cylinder head to corrode.

All the XK engines leak oil to a certain extent, so do not be put off by small dribbles from joint faces here and there. However, beware of major oil leaks at the rear of the engine (the signs will probably be all too apparent, but check again when looking under the car). The problem here will be a failure of the rear main oil seal, which is not an expensive item in itself but which cannot be replaced unless the engine is taken out. Removing the engines from these cars is an awkward operation, not one which can be

Accessibility of most engine components is not too bad, but removing the bonnet makes a distinct improvement if more major work is on the cards. Note that the battery has been removed in this case.

done quickly at home and not one which can be done cheaply by a professional.

All XK engines use a lot of oil by modern standards and the 3.8-litre types are notorious for it. However, excessive oil consumption usually means the valve guides are worn: check for this by having the seller or an assistant rev the engine while you stand behind the car and watch for a cloud of oil smoke as the throttle is released. The denser the cloud, the more urgent is the need to replace those valve guides!

Ask the seller or an assistant to rev the engine up to 1,500rpm and listen for timing-chain rattle. A rattle from the top timing chain will need attention, but is not going to be very expensive. But a rattle from the bottom chain will be bad news because replacement of that chain involves taking the engine out. Tappet noise may also be apparent, but is only cause for concern if it is excessive: clearances can be taken up by relatively simple adjustment.

The Daimler V8 engines should never sound noisy. Like the Jaguar sixes, they should give around 15psi of oil pressure at

Looking rather sorry for itself is this V8 engine from an early Daimler. Restoration should not prove too difficult, however.

idle when hot. Their cooling systems also need a corrosion inhibitor or anti-freeze all year round. Corrosion of the waterways in the cylinder heads is often revealed by leaks; as the cooling system is pressurized, any restriction of the water flow tends to force the pressurized coolant to find its way out of the system somewhere.

However, the Daimler V8 engines are relatively trouble-free and, like the Jaguar sixes, should survive for at least 100,000 miles (160,000km) without a major rebuild. Valve guides are one weak area, and a rattling noise from the top of the engine (not unlike tappet rattle) may indicate that the guides are badly worn. Some engines also seem to suffer from bearing trouble at intervals of 30,000 to 50,000 miles (50,000 to 80,000km), a condition revealed by rumbling noises from the engine's bottom end. The usual problem is wear on the centre three of the crankshaft's five bearings. Less expensive to rectify, although particularly annoying, is misfiring or uneven running. This generally results from neglect of the twin-point distributor.

Other checks for engine condition must be undertaken during a road test of the car and are dealt with later.

IN THE BOOT

A good look inside the boot of a compact Jaguar or Daimler can reveal quite a lot about the car's general structural condition. Most important is to lift the Hardura matting over the rear axle and to check for signs of rust in the corners near and around the damper mountings. The rear springs, Panhard rod and axle trailing arms all mount to the underside of the bodyshell here and corrosion bad enough to show through inside the boot means that the car needs major work and is best left for another buyer.

There may also be rust around the edges of the boot floor, around the exposed inner wheelarches and inside the wings behind the hardboard side panels. None of these need cause real concern, however. Also more of a nuisance than a problem (unless it is very serious) is rust in the spare wheel well. Serious corrosion here is only likely to be found in a generally bad car; light corrosion which has holed the metal needs attention if only to prevent leaks and further rusting, but the spare wheel well is not easy to repair neatly.

UNDERNEATH THE CAR

It is very tempting just to give a cursory look at the underside of a car and then hope for the best; not everybody likes crawling about on the ground to do a more thorough inspection. However, it is absolutely vital to give any compact Jaguar or Daimler a thorough inspection from underneath, because that is the only way to make certain that the bodyshell is sound.

There will be no very serious structural problems at the front of the car, but it is nevertheless important to look for the corrosion damage which does occur. Below the radiator runs a cross-member which is likely to show some rust on almost any car; fortunately, however, it can be repaired fairly easily or even replaced. In more serious cases, rust will also affect the Y-shaped girders which run from near the front bumper mounts to the outriggers. Also worth checking are the support brackets for the front of the wings – known as 'crow's feet' because of their shape – which are often badly rusted but can easily be replaced.

A look under the front wings in passing will confirm any suspicions raised earlier in the inspection that rust may be lurking, ready to break through. It should also

Work on the Daimler engine is relatively straightforward.

afford a good view of the closing panels at the rear of the wings, which suffer from bombardment by road debris and are very often rusty. Replacement is straightforward enough. While under the engine bay, check for leaks from the power steering of cars which have it fitted and double-check for oil leaks from the engine, particularly at the rear main oil seal. Oil leaks from manual gearboxes are not common, but look out for fluid leaks from the Borg Warner DG automatic box: usually, these leaks can only be rectified after removal of the whole transmission.

From the bulkhead backwards is where you must pay special attention, because this is where the structure of the bodyshell is most likely to have been weakened by corrosion. There may be rust in the front of the floorpan, caused by water coming through from the wing-to-body joints. This need not be serious, but any holes here or elsewhere in the floorpan will need attention if the rust is not to spread to more critical areas.

Check particularly the inner sills, the vertical inner surfaces of what appear to be chassis rails running along the outer edges of the floorpan. If they have been repaired, as well they might, make sure that the repair is sound and that new metal has not been welded on simply to disguise corrosion underneath. These sills are vital to the strength of the bodyshell and weaknesses here can make the car unsafe, particularly if it is involved in a collision. For that very reason, weak sills will lead to MoT test failure. Look also at the jacking points at the front and rear of each sill; not only is the area around them a common one for rust to start in the sill itself, but the jacking tubes can also disintegrate. Although remanufactured items are available, they are surprisingly expensive and need to be welded on carefully if they are to bear the weight of the car on a jack during emergency wheel-changing.

The next area to check is the rear of the floorpan, ahead of the rear axle. Here, the rear springs are bolted into channel section members, themselves welded to box section members under the floor. These box sections can actually collapse under the twin attacks of rust and stress, leaving the springs resting against the floorpan without any proper means of attachment to the bodyshell. Corrosion in the centre of the seat pan weakens the attachment points for the trailing arms, which can pull out; further corrosion in this area can also weaken the mounting for the Panhard rod. Do not be surprised to see some localized reinforcement where the Panhard rod mounts to the body: this was a notorious weak spot on the compact Jaguars throughout their production life.

Also worth checking in this area are the springs themselves. It is not unknown for their top leaves to crack or for their front mountings to work loose. If your initial check of the car's appearance showed a list to one side at the rear, now is the time to look for broken leaves or a spring which has become weak with age and is not supporting its side of the car properly. Springs can of course be reset and so weak or broken springs need not be a reason on their own for turning down an otherwise sound car. However, like all work on a compact Jaguar, they cost money – so problems here can be used as a bargaining point to bring the asking price down.

The disc-braked cars have a reputation for poor handbrakes – a reputation which is rather unjustified because problems only arise when maintenance falls below Jaguar's recommended standards. While underneath the car, then, look for stretched or misaligned handbrake cables, and examine the rear brake callipers themselves. Sometimes, the fulcrum bolt associated with the handbrake mechanism seizes: have a look to see whether it is reasonably clean or is caked in grime and therefore likely to be at least partially seized.

Behind the axle, make a further check for rust in the spare wheel well and take a careful look at the fuel tank. Any signs of bad rusting or leaking fuel will be bad news, in any case, but there are two weak spots which deserve a special check. The first of these is at the top towards the front of the car (where leaks will only be apparent if the tank is full). The second is underneath, near the drain plug. Fuel tank repairs are possible, but dismantling is also required, so this can be used as another bargaining point.

ON THE ROAD

Not everybody who is selling a car will allow a prospective buyer to drive it on the road before money has changed hands. The situation will obviously vary from case to case, but it is always better to drive a car yourself if possible. At the very least, a long road-run as front seat passenger should help to reveal faults.

Jaguar seats should be very comfortable and tired examples will give themselves away as soon as you sit in the car. The engine should fire up readily and the hand-brake should release easily. On cars with manual transmission, the clutch pedal should not travel too far before it engages or disengages. Beware of clutch slip, as the engine has to come out before the clutch can be replaced. The gear change is long and quite heavy by modern standards but should not baulk, and growling noises from first gear are quite normal. The absence of synchromesh on bottom gear of the early Moss gearbox will only be apparent when changing down from second to first, usually in traffic. Difficult selection of second probably means that there is a fault with the synchromesh on that gear.

There may be a slight jerk on cars with automatic transmission as you put the car into gear; this is normal, but investigate more serious thumps, such as occur when the engine idling speed is set too high. The automatic gear changes are not as smooth as on more modern transmissions, but they should be clean. Slurred changes or hesitation as the box changes up or down point to wear in the transmission. One cause of such problems may be slipping bands, which can be adjusted; but always remember that some spare parts are hard to find for the early type DG automatic transmissions.

On the move, watch the oil pressure gauge and make sure that it really does register at least 40psi at 3,000rpm when the engine is warm (or between 35 and 45psi on the Daimler-engined cars). Make sure that the engine pulls cleanly from all speeds and listen for strange noises. On the overrun, check in the mirror for any sign of a blue haze behind the car (or, better, have an assistant in a following car look out for it). This haze is oil smoke and indicates that the engine is in need of an overhaul. Be wary, too, of any sloppiness in the handling. This may result from worn subframe mounting rubbers at the front, from wear in the steering, or from nothing worse than worn dampers or tyres. It should be possible to guess at the source of the problem from the feel of the car as it goes round bends.

SUPPORT SERVICES AND CLUBS

Owners of compact Jaguar and Daimler models are among the luckiest in the classic car world, as there is a large support network for the cars. Many mechanical items are shared with other Jaguar and Daimler models, which means demand is high enough for supplies to be maintained and prices to remain reasonable. There is also no shortage of expertise among specialists in the marque to help keep these cars running.

Body panels are more of a problem and complete original panels are now impossible to find. However, some panels (such as Mk 2 front wings) have been remanufactured and repair panels can also be had to suit the areas where rust is most common. Complete remanufactured panels are made in small quantities and are therefore expensive; repair panels are much cheaper but must be fitted by an expert, which of course costs money. The pre-1959 Jaguars are much less well-supported than the Mk 2 and Daimler models, partly because their low survival rate makes remanufacture of panels and repair panels uneconomical. Wings, full spats and door skins are simply not available, and must either be made individually at great expense or adapted from Mk 2 items.

Interior parts can also be refurbished or replaced without too much difficulty, although damaged leather seats will be expensive to repair. Complete retrims cost astronomical sums of money and are best avoided. Often, it is possible to replace damaged seats with better examples from another car, but owners of pre-1959 cars will have difficulty finding another car to cannibalize. Seat trim kits are available for Mk 2s and pre-1967 Daimlers, but owners of other models will have to have upholstery panels or complete covers specially made, which can be very expensive.

The companies which provide support for the compact Jaguars and Daimlers all advertise in the classic car press, and many of them also advertise in the enthusiasts' club magazines. Most specialists are long-established and are keen to protect their good reputations, but from time to time some shadier characters enter the business and try to make a quick killing.

The best way to find out who is trustworthy and who is not is to talk to enthusiasts who have more experience, and the best way to meet them is through the Jaguar and Daimler clubs.

In Britain, there are three separate clubs catering for the compact Jaguars and one for the Daimlers (although these compact Daimlers are also welcomed by the Jaguar clubs as they are fundamentally Jaguar models). The Jaguar clubs, longest-established first, are:

The Jaguar Drivers' Club, Ltd
18 Stuart Street
Luton
Bedfordshire LU1 2SL
Tel: (01582) 419332

The Jaguar Enthusiasts' Club, Ltd
Sherborne Mead Road
Stoke Gifford
Bristol BS12 6TS
Tel: (0117) 969 8186

The Jaguar Car Club
19 Eldorado Crescent
Cheltenham
Gloucestershire GL52 2PY

The Daimler club, which is perhaps better suited to those whose interests also embrace other (pre-Jaguar) Daimlers, is:

The Daimler and Lanchester Owners'
    Club
The Oak House
Gamlingay
Bedfordshire
Tel: (01767) 82563

There are also Jaguar clubs in several other countries, particularly in Europe and in the USA. Their addresses can be obtained from the classic car press.

THE MODERNIZED MK 2

The Mk 2 Jaguar became a favoured classic during the boom years of the late 1980s and early 1990s, and the prices of cars in excellent condition leapt upwards. This in turn led to a boom in the restoration business, as it became financially feasible to spend large sums on restoring a car to as-new condition and to realize a profit when selling the car on. In the wake of this, two companies saw the possibility of rebuilding cars to as-new condition but with subtle alterations to give them many of the advantages of more modern machinery. These companies were Vicarage Jaguar in the UK and Beacham in New Zealand.

The principle behind both companies' work was similar. Bodyshells – generally sound ones rather than rusted-out examples – would be stripped to bare metal and shot-blasted, and then new metal would be let in where necessary and panels in poor condition would be replaced. Priming, painting and a rebuild then followed. Cars could be rebuilt either to pure original condition or updated in certain subtle ways.

Additional performance could be had from fitting a more modern 4.2-litre XK engine. Transmission upgrades were also available, in the Beacham case by means of a five-speed Getrag gearbox. Steering could also be modernized, by fitting the rack-and-pinion system from a Jaguar XJS,

A trial fitting of chrome parts on the restored and painted bodyshell of a Daimler 2.5-litre V8.

while it was also possible to fit ventilated disc brakes for additional stopping power. Other options included uprating the headlamps with halogen units. Naturally, these updates were extra to the cost of the 'standard' ground-up restoration, and did not come cheaply. Sadly, few of these upgraded Mk 2s have ever seen the everyday use for which their revised specification makes them ideal.

Something just a little different ... the Daimler V8 engine is well-liked in the custom-car world as a compact and powerful powerplant which also looks good. This one has been fitted with a supercharger.

Appendix: Building the Compact Jaguars

With the exception of a few thousand cars built overseas from KD (Knocked-Down) kits, all the compact Jaguars were assembled at Jaguar's Browns Lane factory. The build sequence was the same from the beginning of Mk.1 production in 1955 to the end of Daimler V8-250 production fourteen years later.

Every compact Jaguar started life with the arrival at Browns Lane of a variety of components bought in from outside companies. The largest of these was the bodyshell, which was delivered as a bare metal shell from Pressed Steel. Major components bought in included the Moss gearbox (before 1965), the Laycock overdrive and the Borg Warner automatic transmission, while other component suppliers provided smaller items such as bumpers, door handles, tyres, glass and a variety of electrical components.

Immediately after delivery, these components were put into various stores which fed different areas of the main assembly track. The bodyshell went straight to the preparation area of the Paint Shop, while running-gear elements were taken to an area close to the beginning of the Main Assembly Track. Castings for the cylinder heads and cylinder blocks, meanwhile, went to the Machine Shop where they were machined and prepared for assembly into complete engines.

THE MECHANICAL ELEMENTS

Engine build was carried out in a sub-assembly area shared with the assembly tracks for the other Jaguar models, and completed engines were then moved into a further sub-assembly area where they met up with gearboxes. Each gearbox was bench-tested before being bolted to its engine, and then engine and gearbox were filled with oil and subjected to a further bench test which lasted several hours. The oil was then drained, engine and gearbox were refilled with fresh oil, and the assembly passed into the Main Assembly area.

Meanwhile, the front suspension and steering components were being bolted to their subframe in another sub-assembly area. They were fed to the start of the Main Assembly Track, together with completed rear axle assemblies. One front suspension assembly and one rear axle would then be positioned on special jigs on the moving assembly line, which held them the same distance apart as they would be on the fully-assembled car. The jigs then moved with the line to the next assembly area, where engine and gearbox units were lowered on to the front subframe and bolted into position. Next came the propshaft, which was bolted to the rear axle and to the gearbox to link front and rear ends of the car's mechanical 'skeleton'.

Bodies going through the paint shop at Browns Lane were mounted on trolleys so that they could be rotated through 360 degress. In the foreground are Mk 1 2.4-litre shells, emerging from the spray booth. To the left is an unpainted 3.4-litre shell.

A little further down the line, the painted bodyshells are checked for flaws. After being inverted to aid drying, they are turned the right way up for the white-coated inspector on the left of the picture. Note the two-tone Mk VIII saloon on the right.

The scene at the body drop, or 'Clapham Junction' as it was known. The bodyshells, now wearing lights and some chrome trim, are lowered carefully on to the trolley bearing the axles, suspension and power train. Like the two previous pictures, this one dates from 1957.

Work continues on the assembly track. This picture shows Mk 2 models being fitted with headlamps. Note the protective cloth on the wings, to prevent the freshly-painted bodies from becoming scratched.

Mk 2 bodies proceed down the Trim Line, where seats and other interior items will be fitted. The seat cushions are brought to the line side by overhead conveyors.

Nearly there! A 2.4-litre Mk 1, now lacking only bumpers, sidelights and hubcaps, receives its final polish.

BODYSHELLS

While all this was taking place in one area of the factory, the bodyshells which had been delivered to the Paint Shop were mounted on frames which allowed them to be rotated through 360 degrees. After a careful inspection, each shell was then hand-finished and passed into a washing and phosphating plant. Next, it was dipped into a tank of primer to give additional pro-tection to the lower body areas, and moved on to receive two coats of surface primer.

The shells were then rotated so that sound-deadening material could be sprayed onto their undersides, and moved on to the next area where they were rubbed down and sealed. A trip through the baking oven followed, and the bodies were then allowed to cool down before being hand-sprayed with three coats of synthetic enamel colour coat. They passed through a final baking

Mk 2 saloons approach the end of the line. On the right is the Trim Line for the Mk X models. Jaguar's drive for quality is evident in the banners overhead: 'Quality is vital to us all', 'Poor quality stops tracks' and 'Poor quality causes hold ups'.

oven, were allowed to cool down once again and were then given a final inspection before being passed for onward transmission to the Body Assembly Track.

In this next assembly area, the fully painted bodies were fitted out with wiring looms, insulating felt, door and window catches, windscreens and rear windows, instrument panels (fed in from a sub-assembly area where they had been pre-wired) and other items such as radiator grilles.

BODY MEETS RUNNING GEAR

Until this point, the car's running gear and its body had been on two separate tracks. They now met up for the first time as the bodyshells were lifted up and over the track carrying the running gear, and then lowered into position for the two assemblies to be bolted together. (Although the body drop presented no problems for 2.4-litre models with the original Solex carburettors, there

Finished! Completed 2.4-litre and 2.4-litre Mk 1s await their turn for despatch at Browns Lane in 1957.

was insufficient clearance when SUs were fitted later in production, and the carburettors had first to be removed and then refitted after the body was in position!) Further along the line, items such as the bumpers and steering wheel were added, and then last of all the car met up with its wheels - already shod with tyres in another sub-assembly area. With all four wheels in place, the cars came off the end of the Main Assembly Track. Petrol was now put into their tanks and they were started up and driven to the Trim and Finish Track.

All the wood trim for the car's interior, the leather (or, later Ambla) for the seats and the vinyl leathercloth for the door trims had meanwhile been cut to shape in sub-assembly areas alongside this line. Seats, carpets, door trims and wood were now all installed into the cars, which were essentially complete by the time they reached the end of the track.

ROAD TESTS

The next stage was a further inspection – Jaguar achieved their high build standards by employing one inspector for every nine assembly workers – after which each car was taken out for a road test of 30 miles or more to check for defects. On return, they passed to the Service Bay for defect rectification as necessary and for final tuning. They were then taken out on road test a second time, this time by a different tester. Further defect rectifiction followed if necessary, together with a painstaking body inspection, and then the interior was vacuum-cleaned and brushed out. Each car was then hand-polished before going through a final visual inspection and passing on to the Despatch Area. From there, cars were transported to dealers at home or abroad.

Index

PART 2
THE COMPACT DAIMLERS AND
JAGUARS